# Teaching Young Children
# Social Studies

# Teaching Young Children
# **Social Studies**

## Gayle Mindes

Rowman & Littlefield Education
*Lanham • New York • Toronto • Plymouth, UK*

Published in the United States of America
by Rowman & Littlefield Education
A Division of Rowman & Littlefield Publishers, Inc.
A wholly owned subsidary of The Rowman & Littlefield Publishing Group, Inc.
4501 Forbes Boulevard, Suite 200, Lanham, Maryland 20706
www.rowmaneducation.com

Estover Road
Plymouth PL6 7PY
United Kingdom

*Teaching Young Children Social Studies*, by Gayle Mindes, was originally published in
hard cover by Praeger, an imprint of Greenwood Publishing Group, Inc., Westport, CT.
Copyright © 2006 by Gayle Mindes. Paperback edition by arrangement with Greenwood
Publishing Group, Inc. All rights reserved.

British Library Cataloguing in Publication Information Available

The hardback edition of this book was previously cataloged by the Library of Congress as
follows:

Mindes, Gayle.
   Teaching young children social studies / Gayle Mindes.
     p. cm. (Teaching Young Children, ISSN 1554–6004)
   Includes bibliographical references and index.
   1. Social sciences—Study and teaching (Early childhood)—United States. I. Title.
II. Series.
   LB1139.5.S64M56 2006
   372.83—dc22        2006021054
   ISBN-13: 978-0-275-98228-7 (cloth : alk. paper)
   ISBN-10: 0-275-98228-9 (cloth : alk. paper)
   ISBN-13: 978-1-57886-700-4 (pbk. : alk. paper)
   ISBN-10: 1-57886-700-4 (pbk. : alk. paper)

To my family and friends with big ears and bigger hearts . . .

With many thanks, gayle

# Contents

Foreword *by Doris Fromberg*                                                ix

Preface                                                                     xi

1. Introduction to the Power of Social Studies                              1

2. Moral Development, Character Education, and the Social
   Studies                                                                  19

3. Teaching and Learning Social Studies in the Age of State
   Standards and Head Start Outcomes                                        39

4. The Context of Culture in Teaching Social Studies: Beyond the
   Antibias Curriculum *by Leslie R. Williams and Gayle Mindes*            61

5. Perspectives on Positive Classroom Practices *by Linda Davey
   and Doris Pronin Fromberg*                                               79

6. Multimedia, the World, and Young Children                                101

7. Assessing the Accomplishment of Learning in the Social
   Studies                                                                  129

8. Knitting It All Together                                                 145

Appendix: Children's Literature Organized by National Council of
Social Studies Themes *Prepared by Nichole Meier*                          185

Index                                                                       193

# Foreword

Doris Fromberg

If meaning is the center of learning, then social studies sits at the center of content in education. The study of social life and learning about the social sciences is a natural realm in which to integrate a variety of disciplines.

This comprehensive book fulfills the promise of social studies as an integrator of knowledge and the experiences of young children by presenting the broad scope of the social studies field. The field of social studies resides in a time when meaning sometimes takes a back seat to isolated drills. Dr. Mindes deals not only with defining the field but also with relating it to current issues concerning standards-based and skills-based movements. She also provides many strategies, activities, and resources for teachers to use with young children. Both meaningful content and the tools of the social scientist that are relevant for the young social scientist are included within the scope of this book.

There is particular attention to integrating curriculum in ways that provide culturally relevant instruction for diverse groups of children and that include multicultural educational considerations. Although a focus on meaningful learning is a central characteristic of this book, the discussions and suggestions throughout reflect a sensitivity to developmental concerns about young children.

Thus, this book is both comprehensive and detailed. Its scope encompasses the nature of society and the components of citizenship. It is a book for many seasons and helps illuminate the teaching and learning of social studies for the benefit of young children.

# Preface

At birth, young children begin the exploration of their social world. As infants, toddlers, preschoolers, and young school-agers, they interact with people and the environment to learn about the world and their place in it. Gradually they become community members and acquire the skills to be effective citizens in a democratic society. The precise nature of the learnings and the ways in which they learn about the social world, with its customs and rules for engagement, will depend upon the developmental stage as well as family, child care, and school environment. However, all young children will face the demand of policy makers, who require an enlightened citizenship equipped with the tools for problem solving in the twenty-first century.

Using the processes of social studies, teachers facilitate the acquisition of the tools and concepts appropriate for learning the social studies that will serve young learners lifelong. Such tools are raising questions as well as, gathering, analyzing, discussing, and displaying data. These are the open-ended, inquiry-based learning strategies ideally suited for child investigations of topics and themes that appeal to young children. Example themes developed through the exploration of "big ideas" include the following: Who am I? Where do I live? Who are my family members? How do people travel? The themes are timeless and children explore them in the context of their lives, using their previous knowledge and the currency of their lives now. Thus, Who am I? explored at various ages varies in complexity and is influenced by the cultural context of the learner.

So part of social studies is the academic content of the social studies, which includes the traditional fields of history, archeology, anthropology, sociology, political science, economics, geography, and philosophy. This academic content is appropriately scaled for investigation through learner projects. Investigations might begin with a child question such as Where does my food come from? Using the academic tools appropriate for the age of the child, teachers provide learning environments and activities that will enhance the children's understanding of the fundamental questions that they raise. In the pages that follow, this curricular approach is described and applied. As well, the book shows how to develop and enhance the social aspects of learning as part of the processes of social studies.

This text pulls together the disparate, but intertwined, content of the social studies and discusses the processes of social studies that promote social learning, self-concept development, and character development. Issues of culture, classroom community development, and parent collaboration are other vital aspects of the social studies discussed. It offers an integration of this content and a significant examination of issues underpinning it to provide a whole-child orientation to the curricular area of social studies for young children. The approach recognizes that the themes of social studies—culture, time, continuity, and change; people, places, and environments; individual development and identity; individuals, groups, and institutions; power, authority, and governance; production, distribution, and consumption; science, technology, and society; global connections; and civic ideals and practices (NCSS, 1994)—rely on social interactions and child-constructed meaning to support acquisition of the required academic material proposed by state and national standards. Finally, culture and community are inextricably linked to the teaching and learning of social studies.

The book presents social studies content and processes holistically. Beginning in Chapter 1 with a focus on the historical foundations of the social studies, it goes on with current emphases and the importance for strong consideration of culture in the social development of young children. Chapter 2 continues the elaboration of social development and social learning, with a focus on moral development and character education. In Chapter 3, the focus shifts to the particular strategies and methods that facilitate acquisition of knowledge as well as strategic tools for the exploration of the social world. Chapter 4 picks up the discussion of cultural issues and priorities as these interface with the lives of children and families—moving beyond the antibias curriculum. Global issues are explored in Chapter 5. In Chapter 6, the media and methods of instruction are discussed in practical terms. Chapter 7 focuses on the alignment of assessment practices with curricular goals and interventions. The final chapter discusses bringing the social learning and the social studies content together, with pragmatic examples of lesson and thematic investigation planning.

## Key Features of the Text

- Focus questions, study questions, reflection prompts
- Suggested further readings
- Internet resources to support both teacher and child learning
- An integrated approach to social learning and social studies education
- Examples of holistic instructional approaches

## Acknowledgments

Thanks to the thousands of children, parents, undergraduate and graduate students, and colleagues who have influenced my thinking and practices over the years. In particular, I appreciate the thoughtful ongoing reviews and encouragement of the series editors: Doris Fromberg and Leslie Williams. I value the care and hard work of Nicole Meier, DePaul University teaching candidate, who compiled the children's literature collection organized by the National Council for Social Studies themes. John-Patrick Workman at DePaul University provided conscientious and speedy clerical assistance with support from DePaul University students: Ashleigh Pigusch and Lindsay Vail. The librarians at DePaul found the "unfindable" quickly; I am indebted to them for all the reference assistance. Thanks to my colleagues at DePaul University and early childhood educators elsewhere, including especially Linda Davey, for their assistance and support in discussing the book.

Finally, I am especially indebted to my son, Jonathan, for his neverending support and contribution of his professional, editorial opinions throughout the writing process.

I appreciate the support, encouragement, and vision from Elizabeth Potenza and others behind the scenes at Praeger. For expert copyediting and manuscript assistance, I thank Saloni Jain and the copy editing team at TechBooks.

## CHAPTER 1

# Introduction to the Power of Social Studies

The modern world needs people with a complex identity who are intellectually autonomous and prepared to cope with uncertainty; who are able to tolerate ambiguity and not be driven by fear into a rigid, single-solution approach to problems, who are rational, foresightful and who look for facts; who can draw inferences and can control their behavior in the light of foreseen consequences, who are altruistic and enjoy doing for others, and who understand social forces and trends. (Robert Havighurst, in Cohen, 1972, pp. 346–347)

## Terms to Know

- Social Studies
- Social Knowing
- Theme-based Approach
- Constructivist

## Overview

Early childhood educators agree that the foundation for all curricula in the birth to age 8 range is thorough understanding of child development in a multicultural social context. That is, teachers must understand how children learn to move and navigate physically and how children use fine-motor and gross-motor skills in different ways as they grow. They surely must understand the multiple ways that children communicate with each other, their families, and with the people in child care, school, and community settings. Knowledge of this communication development includes perspectives on the evolution of language, speech, and the development of early literacy skills and competencies. Teachers also concern themselves with the personal and social development of their students.

Where do the social studies fit within this foundational knowledge of child development theories? How then do teachers decide upon the content and processes for day-to-day activities, strategies for implementing a social studies curriculum in programs for the various ages? How do teachers choose important overall goals for the social studies curriculum? What exactly are the social studies? In the book that follows, these important considerations will be explicated. To begin, a consideration of the definition of the social studies precedes the investigation of social studies content and processes in early childhood education.

## Focus Questions

1. What are the social studies and where do they fit in the early childhood curriculum?
2. What is the content of social studies and what are the processes of instruction?
3. What do young children learn through the social studies?
4. How does culture influence development and knowledge?
5. What is the power of social studies in the curriculum?

## Social Studies Explored

The content of social studies emerged at the beginning of the twentieth century as a holistic approach to citizenship education. Policy makers at the time were concerned that large numbers of immigrants coming to the United States were not prepared to live in a democratic society. They would need, according to the policy makers, to be shown how to be citizens. Schools were the best place to ensure that citizenship education began. Thus, historically, social studies content met the educational needs of society for the preparation of citizens. Early policy makers concerned themselves with the curricula of the high school, urging teachers to use the techniques of social science: raising questions and gathering, analyzing, discussing, and displaying data. Elementary schools in the beginning of the 20th Century focused on basic education—reading, writing, arithmetic. As elementary schools trickled the content of social studies down from the high school objectives, i.e. citizenship education and social mores appreciation, teachers read stories about the early formation of the United States and focused on children's development of the virtues exemplified in moralistic stories (such as those in the McGuffey readers).

> The "subject matter" for this school subject was to be drawn from the most influential social sciences of the time—history, geography, and civics—and blended together as one school subject for the purpose of helping children understand our American heritage and acquire the skills and sensitivities basic to constructive participation in our nation's democratic society. (Maxim, 2006, p. 13)

## The Social Studies Defined

The primary purpose for the study of social studies content is "to help young people develop the ability to make informed and reasoned decisions for the public good as citizens in a culturally diverse, democratic society in an interdependent world." Social studies investigations promote "civic competence" and draw upon such disciplines as "anthropology, archaeology, economics, geography, history, law, philosophy, political science, psychology, religion, and sociology, as well as appropriate content from the humanities, mathematics, and natural sciences" (National Council for the Social Studies [NCSS], 1994, p. 3).

In the early childhood years, then, social studies takes place in such diverse activities as when children decide together which imaginary roles to play on the jungle gym, which structure to plan to build in the blocks corner, or how to interact when meeting a person in a wheelchair. As well, social studies take place when young children learn about the community where they live and investigate questions of interest to them using social science techniques.

Social studies content learning also occurs when children observe purchases and deliveries at a supermarket, when they see their parents voting during an election, and when they watch a caregiver consult MapQuest (http://www.mapquest.com/) for the best route to the swimming pool. Curricular investigations of social studies happen in a project-based learning environment that permits children the opportunities to see the shared roles of construction workers at a job site, or the wedding photographs of their grandparents. Children also expand their social learning when they meet and play with children whose first language is different than the one they speak.

Social learning and social studies clearly pervade life in any classroom community. The child care and school experiences in the early years thus help prepare each generation to function as citizens in a civil society. So, the ways in which rules are established in the classroom, the choice of thematic investigations to include ecological conservation or other important societal matters, influence the perceptions that children will have about citizenship.

The primary method for incorporating social studies in curricular activity is investigation of content using the processes of social scientists. In this way children construct understandings, develop skills, and acquire dispositions that serve them as lifelong learners. "Teachers can help children develop social perceptions, social skills, a sense of community, and knowledge by adding props to blocks and other sociodramatic play areas that represent different times and places. Teachers can also add transparent pipes to blocks, water, and 'pouring' areas in ways that support collaborative play" (Fromberg, 2002, p. 87). Teachers also facilitate learning by engaging children in thematic topics derived from their curiosity about the world around them.

## The Curriculum of the Social Studies

As a result, topics for the investigation of social understandings and the content of social studies come from child experience, mandates of various state and federal agencies, and teacher knowledge of the traditional disciplines of the social sciences—history, geography, political science, economics, anthropology, and sociology. In the course of building content knowledge about social studies, children interview elders, visit a variety of community sites, read biographies, stories about people, and observe the interactions of other people. They glean through direct observation and interactions a great deal of information about people and the function of goods and services in their community, as well as much social studies content. In the course of their direct curricular experiences, young children interpret what they see on television. Children increase their vocabulary, see signs and other printed material. They learn to compare quantities, to measure, and to display the results of their various explorations. As well, children consider how their social lives and communities are affected by natural phenomena such as storms and floods.

The tools for social studies inquiries are hypothesis development, data gathering and summarization, as well as interpretative displays and summarization. For preschoolers this can mean investigation of such questions as, How does a letter travel from Cleveland to Peoria? Where does email come from? How come it is still light when I talk on the phone to my grandmother and it is dark where I live?

At the primary age, hypotheses investigated may include questions:

Should families rebuild homes on marshland after they are lost in a hurricane? Where exactly is Iraq? What will happen to families in our community when the plant closes?

Through the investigation of these questions, children will utilize early literacy skills, problem-solving techniques, and the skills of knowledge representation such as pictures, charts, graphs, maps, oral and written presentations. In this way, social studies functions as an integrator of curriculum.

## Social Studies as Curricular Integrator

Building on real-life experiences, the study of social studies facilitates young children's knowledge of the social world as well as influences their capacity to function socially and emotionally in the classroom and the world at large. Often, social studies investigations begin with a profound current event that perplexes adults and shakes the very foundations of child life. Consider, for example, the following:

It is September 13, 2001, in a New Jersey public school. Nolan, age $6\frac{1}{2}$, sits at his seat in his first-grade classroom. He is a vivacious and talkative child, yet he now is quiet and he stares vacantly ahead. Nolan knows something is terribly wrong in his world. The Twin Towers have fallen down and it had something to do with "bad men on planes"—but he has seen those buildings and cannot comprehend how they could fall down. They are so big. He knows that several of his friends are not in school today because they have a parent who will not be coming home from the Twin Towers. He heard his mom crying and talking about the Towers falling on the phone. He also knows his own father is not home. His mother said that Daddy cannot get back from California because no planes are flying, but a part of him is worried:

His father worked in a tall building in New York sometimes too. His Mom has packed the car with supplies and blankets, "just in case," and he isn't too sure of what that means exactly. The teacher notices Nolan's distraction and asks, "Are you OK?" The boy quietly answers, "No." "Are you sick?" she probes. He nods affirmatively and then adds haltingly, as if trying to put this new feeling into words, "I feel sick . . . inside my heart." (Davey, 2001, personal communication)

The ways in which teachers in New Jersey and elsewhere facilitated children's coping in response to this tragic period, paired with parental guidance, and media coverage at the time and currently influence the child's *social knowledge*—"knowing that comes from experiences that build social perceptions, social skills, a sense of community, and knowledge" (Fromberg, 2002, p. 87). More recently, teachers and young children come to understand societal interpretations of the War in Iraq, international tragedies such as the tsunami that struck Thailand, Hurricane Katrina that disrupted children's lives and education in New Orleans and elsewhere. The direct effect of these events on children's social understandings depend in part on the proximity of the event to the immediate lives of children; that is, children in Manhattan, New Jersey, were more likely to know a family member or friend directly affected by 9/11. Young children with relatives in Thailand or those who knew vacationers would be more directly affected by the tsunami than those viewing the events on television. Finally, young children in New Orleans who survived the Superdome experience are more directly influenced by parental attitudes, school responses, and media portrayal of the events as they interpret these major life events.

Thus, young children begin to learn about their social world from birth. The messages they receive in their early years are both vivid and lasting. In the investigation of major life-altering events, as well as the seemingly more mundane explorations, such as, What toys did my grandparents play with? What will happen if they serve tilapia in the school cafeteria? require that teachers facilitate a *theme-based approach* to curriculum—one that addresses broad questions of social understandings and learning. Thus questions appropriately explored such as Who am I? How do people move from place to place? as well as those growing from child experience permit the learner to acquire significant understandings about the world and the way in which it works. This is the approach to curriculum that considers developmentally appropriate practice caveats:

- Build on what children already know.
- Develop concepts and processes rather than focusing on isolated facts.
- Provide hands-on activities.
- Use relevant social studies content throughout the year.
- Capitalize on child interest. (Bredekamp & Copple, 1997)

Such principles tell us that young children understand the world from their particular vantage and build knowledge, skills, and dispositions through their diverse home, community, child care and school experiences.

Such an approach validates that young children learn best from teaching practice that fosters multiple ways of knowing. This approach is informed by integrated interdisciplinary experiences that promote understanding, cooperation, and caring in context, in ways that relate to children's knowledge and experience (Fromberg, 1995, p. 77). While some of the disciplines that make up the social studies may seem complex and beyond the capabilities of young children at first glance, thematic investigation of the social studies applies children's immediate lives and appeals to their imagination.

The traditional content for social studies in the primary grades, as defined by the National Council for Social Studies (NCSS):

- Kindergarten—awareness of self in the social setting
- First grade—the individual in school and family life
- Second grade—the neighborhood
- Third grade—sharing the earth with others in the community. (NCSS, 1984, pp. 376–385)

These same topics are often part of preschool curricula, as well. The depth of investigation varies accordingly. For example, awareness of self in preschool may begin with focuses such as I am a boy or I am a girl. I can play with friends. I live with my family. In kindergarten, the focus builds to include reflection on competencies such as writing, ability to work cooperatively in a group, and so on. In preschool, a study of sharing the earth might revolve around an exploration of Where does the trash go when it leaves the wastebaskets in the center? By third grade, the same topic may explore Why do we need oil? Where in the world is oil located? Why do some people want to drill for oil in Alaska?

Thus, the early childhood curriculum relies less on traditional disciplines, as artificial divisions of knowledge categories—mathematics, literacy, science, social studies, and relies on the insightful teacher to help children make connections to learning. In this way, teachers help young children become effective citizens of the world. Such citizenship, it is important to note, is expected to respect multicultural perspectives and values while helping children find common ground with each other (Edwards & Queen, 2002, p. 19). This approach to social studies provides children with an introduction to the ways of a democratic society as well as guiding them through intrapersonal relationships. In addition, the method provides children with approaches to problem solving such issues as social justice, equality, and world hunger. Examples of this kind of problem-solving investigatory activity incorporates child attention to establishing equitable distribution of scarce resources within the classroom, examination of available public transportation options in the neighborhoods of their city, and the dictation or writing of a position statement on the benefits of recycling the garbage in the classroom, school, home, or community.

For teachers of young children, social studies processes are a way of being with children, as much, if not more, than a subject in the curriculum. This approach considers the *social* part of *social studies* and the "complex social interactions affecting children today—inside and outside the school setting" (Edwards and Queen, 2002, p. 6). Thus, social studies content and processes explore how people can get along and interact with each other in families, groups, classes, communities, and the world in general. This exploration by children of such enduring issues impacts and influences their understanding of the social world. Teachers scaffold child experiences in the social world so that initial encounters with concepts represent first-draft interpretations. For example, several years ago, when Haley's comet was making its once-in-a-century appearance, a teacher arranged a field trip to a campus planetarium. The children were enthralled by the night sky projected on the ceiling. When the astronomer asked them to "call" the comet out, they were delighted that each time they said, "Comet, please come out," the comet tracked across the sky as if on command. These children's memories would initially promote the belief that calling to the comet caused the tracking (Davey, 2005, personal communication).

As the children returned to their classroom, their teacher would then help children understand the nature of comets by reading stories so they could begin foundational knowledge in astronomy. Thus, children use this experiential knowledge and their literacy experiences as they move into their adult years and as they are called on to refine, to interpret, and, ultimately, to protect the democratic principles of U.S. society. "If equality, humanity, and freedom are the promise of democracy, then education is the promise keeper" (Darling-Hammond, 1995, p. 6). In U.S. schools, this "promise keeping" undergirds the social studies curriculum.

## The Critical Intersections of Social Development and the Social Studies

The expectation in the United States is that through social studies curricula, children will also learn aspects of social interaction that include fairness, social justice, and democratic principles; such skills will enable them to become informed and caring citizens. In this sense, the most important element in social studies takes place from the moment a teacher greets a child entering the classroom. For example, consider the following anecdote:

> Noelle is five and she is late for school. Her working mom is away at a conference and everything is out of kilter in Noelle's world. As she approaches her room with a neighbor, she appears obviously anxious and unsure. When the door to the classroom is opened, she sees that her classmates are gathered at the opposite corner of the room, singing with a teaching assistant. The teacher is working with a small group of children on a letter of thanks to the fifth graders who came to read to them yesterday. Noelle hesitates uncertainly at the door. The teacher nods to Noelle and says, Good morning, I am glad you are here today. Please put your coat away and join your friends who are singing. We'll talk in a minute so you can know what we've done so far today. Noelle smiles, puts her coat away and goes to sit by her friend, Qiana. (Davey, 2005, personal communication)

With this experience, Noelle meets an empathetic teacher who recognizes her distress about being late. She provides a graceful way for her to enter the ongoing activities. The other children continue with their activities. Later the teacher will find out why Noelle was late and offer assurances that these things happen. She may ask if Noelle wants to draw a picture for her mother as a gift when she returns. Through these personal interactions, then, Noelle and the other children learn strategies for coping with stress, classroom disruption, and acceptance of momentary or unusual events.

Accordingly, there are many social learnings that children can absorb in the course of daily interactions. For example, children learn to balance self-interest with caring for others. If there is one copper crayon in the class crayon bin, Andy may want to use it to draw the roof of a building. He realizes that Harold is drawing plumbing pipes, so he cares for Harold by handing him the copper crayon and selecting the green one for himself. They learn the responsibilities of ownership as well as the requirements for sharing. For example, Lauren brought a book about babies that Aunt Susan gave her for her birthday. She has protected the book by bringing it in a brown paper bag. The teacher will read the story and classmates will have an opportunity to read it throughout the day. Children experience opportunities to empathize with others as well as opportunities to become independent and self-motivated. For example, Loreta drops the utility ball in the circle game on the playground almost every time it is thrown to her. Brian starts to laugh and say something like, Loreta you are such a dork. Damien reminds Brian that he, Brian, dropped the ball several times yesterday and that it is rude to laugh and call others names. As part of a thematic investigation of families, Tricia draws a family tree, Lee cuts photos of family members and places them on a picture of a tree, while Avery uses the computer and Kidspiration software to complete the depiction of his family tree. As sensitive teachers promote social learnings in the daily life of the classroom, they must consider the cultural context of the classroom, as well and the diverse family experiences that determine family perceptions of the obligations of citizenship and the principles of democracy.

## Cultural Contributions in the Investigation of Social Studies

Just as we commonly assume that young children come to early childhood programs with a personal set of skills, concepts, and ways of behaving, children bring to school their interpretations of their familial and community social experiences in the community. That is, they bring the concepts of appropriate behavior, relationships, and habitual ways of exploring based on their experiences in their families and in the community. In addition, young children bring various understanding of their social world through their personal lens of culture.

One definition of *culture* is

the totality of socially transmitted behavior patterns, arts, beliefs, institutions, and all other products of human work and thought. These patterns, traits, and products considered as the expression of a particular period, class, community, or population: *Edwardian culture; Japanese culture; the culture of poverty*. These patterns, traits, and products considered with respect to a particular category, such as a field, subject, or mode of expression: *religious culture in the Middle Ages; musical culture; oral culture*. [Culture is the] predominating attitudes and behavior that characterize the functioning of a group or organization. Intellectual and artistic activity and the works produced by [a culture]. (*American Heritage Dictionary of the English Language*, 2004)

Frequently in classrooms across the country, culture and the implications of diversity is reduced to a consideration of the food, art, crafts, music, and clothing that serve as identifying codes for separating and sorting people by simple observable signifiers. This surface view of culture misses the richness of cultural influences that enriches people's lives. A closer look at culture might choose to examine a particular group's history or race, tying in such activities as common geography, language, class, and traditions. This view also tends to rely on outside indicators that may or may not represent a true picture of diversity (Ramsey, 2004).

Looking beyond and expanding such arbitrary surface divisions of culture is viewed as the way a group of people commonly understand their world; how they think, feel, and act; what they value; how they behave; what they honor; and what they believe (Hollins, 1996). This view of culture opens the door for understanding the complexity of family and self-definition of culture that transcends external, arbitrary ascriptions by others and the requirements for static definitions of culture, permitting the family to pick and choose the attributions of traditional cultural definitions as well as those gained through interactions with dominant cultures in a society. As well, those who come from a dominant culture, situationally defined, come to understand the disparate views of specific "other" cultures.

Thus, in trying to understand the children in our early childhood programs, we must note that children's individual experience occur through the interactions between adults and children in "specific cultural contexts or situations" (DeGaetano, Williams, & Volk, 1998, p. 46). Culture here is meant to include not only differences among children and their families, but also the teachers' "ethnicity, gender, race, economic class, religion, abilities and disabilities, age, sexual orientation, and experiences" (DeGaetano et al., 1998, p. 46). Consequently, the ways in which cultural factors influence a teacher's planning for and interaction with children is an essential ingredient in the choices that teachers make in support of optimal learning and teaching for all children. This is a view of diversity that moves beyond a focus on the externals of a child's or a teacher's culture and addresses the complexities of the forces that affect every individual social action and interactions among and across children with different cultural experiences. From this perspective, diversity is described as "encompassing the domain of human characteristics that affect an individual's capacity to learn from, respond to, or interact in a social environment" (Ducette, Sewell & Shapiro, 1996, p. 324). When teachers recognize that learning is so inextricably tied to a respect for diversity and culture, they begin to see why in-depth definitions are important in order to help meet the needs of the young child.

Unfortunately, the failure to recognize and appreciate the dynamic nature of cultural influences on children's learning leads to misconceptions that can intrude into many early childhood programs. This occurs even in programs that strive to implement diverse perspectives without considering the complexities involved. Three approaches that are common but inappropriate are the European American culture–centered (focuses on a single culture, such as "Irish"), the difference denial (sees everyone as alike and therefore soon takes on an European American face, such as everyone celebrates a holiday in December), and multicultural (addresses differences as an "add-on" not truly integrated into the curriculum, e.g., "let's make latkes in December or read a poem about Rosa Parks in February's Black History month"; (Bredekamp & Rosengrant, 1999). These well-meaning but misplaced efforts are in contrast to instruction that is expressed in an overarching orienting concept for understanding cultural processes as "humans develop through their changing participation in the social activities of their communities, which also change" (Rogoff, 2003, pp. 3–4). This concept lays the mental framework for interpreting culture as not just what other people *do*, but understanding one's own cultural heritage, as well as other cultural communities. The approach requires taking the perspective of people of contrasting backgrounds, recognizing that particular cultural practices fit together and are connected. As well, this perspective respects that cultural communities continue to change, as do individuals. Finally, there is not likely to be *one best way* (Rogoff, 2003, pp. 11–12).

In addition to respecting the complexity of cultural understandings as these impact teachers' work with children, teachers' interactions with parents are a critical component for respecting diversity and difference. "Anyone who works with other people's children—for instance, as a teacher, child care provider or social worker—should understand the values and goals of the parents of those children. [Teachers] should examine their own behaviors to see whether what they are doing with the children, or with the families, is in harmony with what the families want for themselves and their children. Recognizing that cultural learning starts at birth and is mostly nonverbal, it is imperative that those who work with families familiarize themselves with cultural differences" (Gonzalez-Mena, 2002, p. 104).

Finally, in another definitional understanding of the term culture are the trends that influence societal perceptions and activities, i.e. popular culture.Teachers recognize that popular culture is always changing. These changes are reflected in, for example, the toys and media of a generation—Barbie Dolls, GI Joe, Power Rangers, Spongebob Squarepants, and so on. As well, sports and games played differ by generationsor by cultural traditions. For example, is it soccer, baseball, football, lacrosse or rugby that consumes the interests of children? In addition, books, movies, and art of popular culture vary by generation. For example, is it Mickey Mouse, Toy Story, or Harry Potter that permeate the interests of families and children?

Inventions transform society and cultures—the printing press, the automobile, shopping malls, Post-it notes. Throughout history, as industrial and technological advances occur, inventions tend to trickle down from the innovators, throughout the adult community members to children. Today, advances related to technology are implemented, in many cases, by the children in our society before these are woven into the popular cultural life experiences of the adults around them. Children navigate the Internet, play video games, and use iPods, cell phones, as well as other digital gadgets with an aplomb, creativity, and confidence that sometimes leave some adults around them baffled. They experiment and pick up the new "language" with ease. Thus, the technologically influenced popular culture requires that teachers consider appropriate inclusions of technology in the social studies curriculum as a measure of societal impact, as tools to enhance the personalization of learning, and as phenomena that transforms the very way in which knowledge develops.

## The Power of Social Studies in the Early Childhood Curriculum

What, then, do the processes and content of social studies offer the early childhood curriculum? "Social studies as content and process is a vibrant and vital part of early childhood curricula. Social studies at the center of early childhood curricula offers the hope that the focus of education will be on the development of effective, efficient, ethical children who will approach their world nonsimplistically and thoughtfully. With the help of good teachers, children will not only absorb the content that focuses on citizenship education in all its permutations but also learn how to learn and how to consider multiple perspectives" (Mindes, 2005, p. 17). This view of the power of social studies is explicated in the following pages of this book.

Specifically, social studies investigations in early childhood offer opportunities for children and teachers to develop rules and structure to support social learning, to build a sense of community, to attend to a culturally relevant pedagogy that focuses on a global human rights perspective and appreciates the virtues that sustain a moral approach to learning. To implement the social studies curriculum in early childhood programs, teachers organize learning through a theme-based approach that sets the stage for learning using toys, texts, literature, symbols, as well as video, computer, and other mass media. In this approach to teaching, assessment is aligned to curricular goals, and the measurement of learning relies on an understanding of the day-to-day application of performance-based assessment. Such an approach focuses on thinking, creativity, and a *constructivist* view of learning, or that it is the learner who constructs or develops new knowledge by actively pursuing the understanding of concepts in light of the learner's previous experiences. It is the teacher who knows the learners in a class who provides diversified learning opportunities for the particular children. Teaching and learning is thus inquiry-based—built on the curiosities of the learners. The power of a vital early childhood social studies curriculum goes beyond the antibias curriculum to a forthright understanding of the complexities of a diverse society, with considerations of social class and power relationships in our society as these affect the lives of children and their families, as well as the early childhood programs that serve them.

## Summary

This chapter presented a definition of social studies, a brief history of the field, and a preview of ways to incorporate social studies investigation in early childhood programs. An overview of the dynamic, inquiry-based social studies curriculum featuring a holistic and thematic approach to teaching and learning is previewed. Social learning resulting from a holistic approach to social studies curricular implementation is described. Important ways that teachers and children use their social interactions to acquire knowledge and dispositions is illustrated. In addition, the chapter highlighted the imperative need to respect, understand, and consider cultures from the perspectives of families and children. Finally, the chapter featured a preliminary description of technology as a product of culture, as well as a tool and influencer of the social studies curriculum.

## Activities in the Field

1. Interview several teachers who are working with groups of various ages. Ask about the cultural composition of the class. Find out how they meet parents at the beginning of the year. Learn how they incorporate culture diversity in their programs. Discuss your findings with your colleagues.

2. Visit a local elementary school. Ask teachers at various grade levels how they incorporate social studies in the classroom. In your notebook, sketch room arrangements. Note bulletin board displays. Discuss your findings with your colleagues.

3. Think back to your childhood experiences with technology. What kinds did you use at different stages of your development? What technological tools do you use as a college student? How does your reflection match what you see in schools and child care centers?

## Activities in the Library

1. Review the last several issues of *Social Studies and the Young Learner* and of *Young Children*. Which social policy issues are discussed? What are some of the curricular and instructional strategies highlighted in these journals? How will you use your findings in planning social studies for your class?

2. In a curriculum library at your college or public library, look at the materials available for use with children. Think about the materials available when you were a child. How do the materials compare? What issues or topics do you see in modern materials? Which issues and topics might be missing? Discuss your findings with your colleagues.

## Study Questions

1. In your own words, what is social studies?
2. What is the content and what are the processes of social studies?
3. What is the curriculum of the social studies in the early years?
4. How are activities structured for social studies? What is your preliminary understanding of theme-based and constructivist approaches to education?
5. What do children learn from social studies?
6. How do your own cultural understandings and the cultural backgrounds of young children and their families affect social studies education?
7. What is the power of social studies in early childhood?

## Reflect and Re-read

1. How do young children learn social studies?
2. What did policy makers want to accomplish in the past through social studies education? What do you believe current policy makers are emphasizing related to social studies?

3. Is children's play and children's literature a powerful way for children to learn about the social world?

## Suggested Readings

DeVries, R., & Zan, B. (1994) *Moral classrooms, moral children: Creating a constructivist atmosphere in early education.* New York: Teachers College Press. A thorough explication of the sociomoral atmosphere of class community development.

Edwards, B., & Queen, J. (2002). *Using multicultural literature to teach K-4 social studies.* Boston, MA: Allyn & Bacon. Children's literature selections are excellent vehicles for child learning about the social studies.

Hall, S. (2000). *Using picture storybooks to teach character education.* Phoenix, AZ: Oryx Press. This excellent reference links current events to character education.

Herr, J., & Libby-Larsen, Y. R. (2004) *Creative resources for early childhood classroom* (4th ed). Clifton Park, NY: Delmar Thomson. A reference for activities to use as starting point in thinking about many themes that may be of interest to your class.

## References

### Books

*The American heritage dictionary of the English language* (4th ed.). (2004). New York: Houghton Mifflin Company.

Bredekamp, S. & Copple, C. (1997). *Developmentally appropriate practice in early childhood programs, revised edition.* Washington, DC: National Association for the Education of Young Children.

Bredekamp, S., & Rosengrant, T. (Eds.). (1999). *Reaching potentials: Transforming early childhood curriculum and assessment.*

Cohen, D. H. (1972). Beyond the home to school and community. In R. Havighurst (Ed.), *The learning child.* New York: Pantheon.

Darling-Hammond, L. (1995). *Education for democracy.* Inaugural lecture as William F. Russell Professor in the Foundations of Education, January 26, 1995.

DeGaetano, Y., Williams, L. R., & Volk, P. (1998). *Kaleidoscope.* Upper Saddle River, NJ: Merrill.Ducette, J. P., Sewell, T. E., & Shapiro, J. P. (1996). In F. B. Murray (Ed.), *The teacher educator's handbook: Building a knowledge base for the preparation of teachers* (pp. 323–380). San Francisco: Jossey-Bass.

Edwards, B., & Queen, J. (2002). *Using multicultural literature to teach K-4 social studies.* Boston, MA: Allyn & Bacon.

Fromberg, D. P. (2002) *Play and meaning in early childhood education.* Boston: Allyn & Bacon.

Fromberg, D. P. (1995). *The full day kindergarten: Planning and practicing a dynamic themes curriculum* (2nd ed.). New York: Teachers College Press.

Gonzalez-Mena, J. (2002). *The child in the family and the community* (3rd ed.). Upper Saddle River, NJ: Merrill/Prentice Hall.

Hollins, E. (1996). *Culture in school learning: Revealing the deep meaning.* Mahwah, NJ: Erlbaum.

Mindes, G. (2005). Social studies in today's early childhood curricula. *Young Children*, 60(5), 12–18.

Ramsey, P. (2004) *Teaching and learning in a diverse world, third edition*. New York: Teachers College Press. Rogoff, B. (2003). *The cultural nature of human development*. Oxford: Oxford University Press.

## Web Sites

Children's Defense Fund. http://www.childrensdefense.org/. An advocacy organization that promotes the welfare of young children and their families. A source for facts and figures about the lives of children as well.

National Association for Multicultural Education. http://www.nameorg.org/. This association promotes understanding of cultural issues as they apply to education and contains links to publications and resources for teaching.

National Association for the Education of Young Children. http://naeyc.org/. The association that advocates for the interests of young children. Many resources and links for policy and practical concerns of teachers.

National Council for Social Studies. http://www.ncss.org/. The association that promotes the teaching and learning of social studies with resources and publications related to the social studies.

## CHAPTER 2

# Moral Development, Character Education, and the Social Studies

Character is like a tree and reputation like its shadow. The shadow is what we think of it; the tree is the real thing. Abraham Lincoln (Brooks, 1879, p. 586)

## Terms to Know

- Self-esteem
- School self
- Cognitive self-concept
- Character
- Empathy
- Community building
- Conflict resolution
- Etiquette
- Self-esteem
- Self-efficacy
- Cognitive reciprocity

## Overview

Young children develop a sense of self in a social context. This context includes an orientation to right and wrong and appropriate behavior that begins with their family's values. With school experience, children modify their views of themselves—who they are in the social world. The school experience, beginning at age 2, 3, 4, or 5 influences *character*, which is an individual's approach to ethical issues. In addition, school experiences affect development and facilitate the development of mainstream social behaviors and values. The resolution of self-identity is influenced by the issues of cultural diversity and urban, suburban, and rural environment factors. The curriculum of the social studies plays a pivotal role in the classroom influence on this social development of self. Social development is fostered by respectful teachers, scaffolding of social learning experience, classroom community development, and the inclusion of character education discussions.

## Focus Questions

1. How do children develop self-concept? The social self? The school self?

2. How do teachers and children build classroom community?

3. When should you use a structured approach to social skills development? How do you implement it?

4. What are the complicated relationships among and between family life, school expectations, and diverse cultural beliefs?

5. What is character education and how do you see it in the classroom?

## Self-Concept and the Evolution of Social Studies

Young children begin, of course, to develop a social sense of self through family interactions beginning in infancy. This sense of self is often characterized as *self-esteem*, the pride, or lack of pride, in one's self as an individual. It is this self-esteem or confidence in self that creates the foundation for learning—the will to take risks, to try new things. Self-esteem drives learner curiosity. Besides initiative for self-learning, babies begin learning a sense of social-self—who am I in relation to others. Thus, this sense of the social self begins in the family. It is in child care and educational settings that the social sense of self evolves beyond family, the resolution of self-identity. Contacts with peers, teachers, other center/school personnel, and parents of classmates influence this sense of self. Thus, the *school self* that sees oneself as a learner and a member of a learning and social community begins to emerge.

Through the social studies curriculum, teachers of young children can facilitate important social learning and provide opportunity to understand diversity among peoples. These social understandings build upon the foundation of a *cognitive self-concept*—the picture of self gained through reflection and contemplation of the self's action in response to others; emotional expression of self to others and social–emotional responses from peers and adults, sense of self-esteem, and gender identity lead to *self-efficacy*, or a feeling of competence.

Parental contacts and models, sibling and peer relationships, child care center and school structure, and finally interpersonal interactions with teachers and other center/school personnel moderate both a foundational development of self-concept and the understandings of a *school self*. It is through these interactions that each child understands where learning and school fits into personal life. Very early, children learn to think of themselves as "scholars," "leaders," and "athletes" or, in negative terms, as "dummies," "trouble-makers," and so forth. Thus, as teachers, you must provide individual, respectful interactions with particular students and nurture respectful interactions between and among children, especially as they involve caring and sensitivity to others. When talking with children, as teacher, you model civility with such statements as, "Sharon, please bring me the red crayon." Or, when calling upon children to remember the established rules, you may say, "Stephanie, how do you ask your classmate to help you clean up? Yes, 'David, please help me.'"

Besides learning a sense of self, young children evolve in their perceptions of *empathy*; this is the capacity to see an issue or situation from another's point of view. *From* "Why is she crying?" and the teacher's answer, "She hit her thumb when pounding the nails into the board," *to* "She is crying 'cause her thumb hurts." Young children show empathetic perception. Note the teacher's intervention in facilitating this perception.

One way to help children increase the ability to feel empathy in the primary years includes using stories that pose moral dilemmas. Upright (2002) suggests that teachers first assess with an interview where children are in their development of empathy by asking individuals to define an empathetic behavior such as "kindness." Then, using stories from shared experience or from children's literature, tell or read the story. Make sure that the children understand the story by asking them to tell the story in their own words. Next, ask the children to describe the conflict in the story. Ask questions to promote thinking about the diverse positions implicit in the conflict. Record the answers so you can chart the growth of individuals and the group over time. Sometimes ask the children to write or draw the dilemma from a particular point of view. Accordingly, children may choose to draw the dilemma from the view of, say, the child who knocked the blocks down or from the point of view of the child whose structure was demolished. These lessons are in addition to the teacher's use of the "teachable" moment during day-to-day interactions among and between children (Mindes & Donovan, 2001).

## Classroom Community Building

In these ways, teachers can facilitate social–emotional development and classroom community through lessons and intentional planning. This happens through the careful consideration of a planning baseline (Berry & Mindes, 1993). Components of the baseline include the room arrangement, schedules, routines, rules and expectations, and personal interactions. Attention to the details of the baseline facilitates the flow of students through the room and provides the backbone for academic achievement. Two of the planning baseline components that facilitate classroom community are

- *Rules and expectations* are clearly delineated so that predictable consequences provide security for classroom citizens. Behavioral guidelines reflect the values of the school community. Involving students in the creation and modification of classroom rules ensures the practice of classroom democracy. For example, the third-grade girls say at a class meeting that the boys always grab the utility ball for the outdoor play period. After discussion, boys and girls agree on a rotation schedule for using the ball.

- *Personal interactions* are the ways in which the members of the classroom community interact. These include student–student, teacher–student, and teacher–multiple students exchanges. Teachers choose roles of observer, facilitator—by suggesting or prompting strategies or words for children to use in various classroom activities, leader, stage manager, and participant depending on the goals of the particular lesson.

Therefore, setting the stage for classroom peer interactions is a critical part of fostering social–emotional development of each of the children in a class. An essential ingredient for the *classroom community*—the teacher and students of a given classroom—is mutual respect that is continually practiced across all relationships: child–child, adult–child, and adult–adult relationships observed by children (DeVries, Hildebrant, & Zan, 2000, p. 10).

One way that teachers establish a positive environment is through modeling appropriate verbal exchanges with children and by not permitting children to belittle others explicitly or implicitly. Stanulis and Manning (2002) describe situations where teachers implicitly reinforce stigmatization of children in the following scenarios:

- A new boy, Louis, arrives and the teacher, Miss Pickle, searches for a place for him to sit. When she seats him next to Albert, the children say, "No, not next to Albert." She then moves Louis in front of Albert and Sally says, "Well, that is better than being next to Albert." Through this behavior, Miss Pickle accepts that Albert is someone to avoid and communicates to Louis that she doesn't respect all students. In the same situation, if Miss Pickle says that she will rely on Albert to mentor Louis, she communicates respect for all students.

- Using the storybook *Chrysanthemum* (1996), Ms Mustard helps children understand that names are important to each child and that names are to be respected—not laughed at when children are unfamiliar with them. Ms Mustard might follow up with activities that discover the history of name choice, giving each child an opportunity to share the heritage of their own names.

*Peer competence*, as described by Kemple (2004), is the idea that in the social context of the classroom, young children learn from interactions with peers; therefore, an aspect of fostering social development is fostering young children's capacity to mentor each other. As young children engage with a more diverse repertoire of young children—children with disabilities, children from varying cultures, and children from various incomes—the development of peer mentoring skills and interaction skills will require greater intervention and consciousness on the part of teachers. You can facilitate such development by reflecting on observations and creating effective room arrangements to support collaborative learning and interaction among the peers. Besides the teacher's facilitative role, young children then learn how to support each other. For some issues, a formal structure for resolving conflict or controversy may be desired.

*Class meetings* may be a useful device for the second- and third-graders. Angell (2004) describes one way to conduct these meetings in a formal manner. With the formality, children appreciate the importance of the meetings that she constructs with a student-chair, sergeant-at-arms, and minute-reader.

The minutes include Reminders (that the class has agreed upon at the last meeting) such as "Don't go in people's desks"; Announcements, Questions, Acknowledgments (and Apologies), and Suggestions. Class meeting time is one way to use a formal structure to deal with conflict or controversy.

At younger age levels, class meetings may require less formality and be quite useful for solving classroom problems. For example, a class has a problem with people hitting each other while standing in line. What can we do to solve this problem? With teacher facilitation, children may identify a concrete way to measure increased distance between children standing in line (cf. Vance & Weaver, 2002).

## Rules and Structure to Support Learning

Conflict resolution, an ability to resolve differences with another, is an essential aspect of social and moral development that requires acquisition of skills and judgment to negotiate, and compromise, as well as develop a sense of fairness (Killen, Anlila-Rey, Barakkatz, & Wang, 2000, p. 74). Both teachers and children in preschool perceive that teachers do and should intervene in conflict situations.

Hitting, meanness, hoarding toys, and other moral dilemmas in the classroom require teachers to use direct commands, such as rule statements, explanations, and time-out directives. See Table 2.1 for examples of these instances.

For social-convention transgressions or *etiquette*—which are the rules for social engagement—violations such as not saying "please," "thank you," teachers should use indirect commands such as hints and suggestions (Killen et al., 2000, p. 74) as well as modeling. Etiquette violations

**Table 2.1**
**Teacher's Commands, Rule Statements, and Time-out Directives**

| | |
|---|---|
| Command | Russell, stop running now. |
| Rule statement | Sue, please use your 3-inch voice when working with Clara. |
| Time-out directives | Kathryn, you may sit in the time-out chair until you are ready to work cooperatively with Ronald. |

are subject to cultural interpretation, however, and so teachers need to be aware of the etiquette standards for the cultures represented in the class. At the same time, part of the social studies curriculum is explaining conventional etiquette observed in the U.S. mainstream. "Manners are minor morals. They are the everyday ways we respect other people and facilitate social relations. They make up the moral fabric of our shared lives" (Lickona, 2004, p. 166).

One way to help children learn these conventions is through the explicit description of "school behavioral expectations." Thus, you may say: "You know at school we say 'excuse me' when we accidentally knock a paper from Gerald's desk." Or "When you come to school, it is like going to someone's home, so you say: 'Good morning, Ms Antelope.' When you leave, you say 'See you later, Bye'" (Lickona, 2004). With this approach, you have conveyed that "school'" has certain etiquette conventions.

A focus on "at school" can communicate to children that different social settings have different conventions and that children can have a repertoire of social conventions to use in various settings. One way to ensure that children understand both the moral imperative of respect for the human rights of their classmates and others, as well as the etiquette conventions, is to involve the children themselves in identifying rules and standards for behavior.

Teachers can work with children to develop rules as convictions about "right" behavior emerge. DeVries et al. (2000, pp. 20–22) give examples arising from practice where some children are concerned about others' treatment of the class guinea pig. The class then makes rules, for example:

- Ask the teacher before you take the guinea pig out.
- Be careful—no hurting the guinea pig.
- Don't squeeze, drop, or throw him. Hold him gently.
- Don't put him on the floor. Hold him.

In another situation, children are hurting each other. Through the discussion, children develop rules such as the following:

- Use your words.
- No hitting.
- No kicking.
- No fighting.
- Don't hurt anyone.

When children forget the rules, discussion or prompting can help them remember their own rules. An example of a classroom rule is, "No touching people when they say no." "He touched me." "What are you going to do? Tell him No" (DeVries et al., 2000, pp. 23–24).

## Classroom Provisions That Model Respect and Build a Sense of Community

Stone (2001) suggests a very broad approach to demonstrate "respect" for children that includes an appropriate daily schedule and a safe and comfortable environment where children can learn and be engaged in many rich learning experiences. The teacher's respect for children leads to planning a balanced curriculum with fresh updates throughout the year. This is a curriculum that considers and "respects" children, with the following attributes:

*Room arrangement*—having traffic patterns that match the classroom activities planned. Learning centers are clearly set up and defined by topic, with appropriate space to match the activities. Equipment and materials are accessible and grouped to encourage child management of them.

*Schedule*—reflects balance of individual, small-group, and large-group activity structure. A well-developed schedule includes large blocks of time during the week to support theme-based curricular endeavors.

*Routines*—facilitate efficient accomplishment of everyday tasks and promote a sense of structure and predictability about the days and weeks of school. These include activities such as collecting lunch money, distributing papers, lining up, and reporting attendance. (Berry & Mindes, 1993)

Finally, words and tone of voice are other ways that teachers communicate an atmosphere of respect for children.

## Providing a Supportive Structure to Develop Social Skills

While most young children will acquire social skills through the natural process of personal interactions with family, friends, teachers, and schoolmates, some children will require more structure. This is just as some children need to have learning tasks carefully sequenced with many concrete, individual steps outlined. One approach to this process is the Stop and

Think Social Skills Program (Knoff, 2001). The program organizes social skills into four sets:

1. Survival skills—listening, following directions, ignoring distractions, speaking up for self
2. Interpersonal skills—sharing, waiting for a turn, joining an activity
3. Problem-solving skills—asking for help, apologizing, deciding what to do, accepting consequences
4. Conflict-resolution skills—handling teasing, losing, peer pressure

Whether through a structured approach for particular children or the relationships in a supportive classroom, the goal for teachers and schools is to build and elaborate social skills. These are the skills that foster a child's sense of empathy, and help to develop conflict-resolution approaches, self-control that ensures mood regulation, and the ability to delay gratification or wait. One way to facilitate these skills is through fantasy play; this is the kind of play that permits children to take on roles in scenarios or through stories created or remembered. It permits children an opportunity to try out new behaviors and roles without risking loss of status or face in a "real" situation. Singer's (1973) research on parents and children documents that children who engaged highly in fantasy play had a greater capacity for waiting patiently, attributable to their parents' having engaged in fantasy play with them. However the skills are developed, the most important yield is that these skills help build a sense of self-efficacy, a belief that personal goals are achievable and under a modicum of control by the particular child.

## Culturally Relevant Pedagogy and Issues of "Hidden Curricula"

In our increasingly global society, children and parents frequently come with different cultural experiences than their teachers and often the classmates are from diverse backgrounds. These cultural differences influence child rearing traditions as well as child behavior and communication styles that come to school. For culture includes the history, values, beliefs, and current political reality for each group.

Mainstream U.S. culture is often described as youth-oriented, future-oriented, materialistic, and clock-conscious. Individuals are expected to be self-reliant and the shared understanding among U.S. citizens is that everyone has a chance to shoot for the top. Not all cultures share these values and approaches to life. As well, many people in this country have been affected by the false promises of mainstream values, for example, that everyone has a chance at elite colleges. However, schools that are underfunded often produce graduates with limited curricular exposure to the college preparatory curriculum or the guidance they need to attempt the admission process.

Cultural beliefs influence family choices about meals, bedtime, gender roles, child discipline, and expectations of teachers and schools. For immigrants, acculturation "to the mainstream United States" varies from keeping one's traditional practices, those from their country of origin, to a dualistic approach that includes embracing both a traditional and an individualistic approach that favors neither traditional nor mainstream U.S. culture (Ramirez & Casteneda, 1974). Others describe acculturation as more fluid and mosaic, that is, the role of cultural identity for individuals and families may be in process or may change in response to individual and family experiences. Thus, teachers must take their cues from families about traditions in the home rather than ascribing stereotypical cultural characteristics to individuals and families.

Nevertheless, it is important to show your support for diversity with the following items in your classroom:

- Photos of people from the community, state, region, and other countries
- Music of various forms
- Children's books from diverse cultural groups
- Texts and other materials that follow antibias principles

While culture influences all of the ways that children behave, schools have relied on definitions of social expectations that are typically related to the dominant culture, such as the following:

- Social space—arm's length away
- Authority of the teacher
- Time—exact adherence
- Rules—developed by teachers
- Language—standard English

- Competition
- Privilege for alphabetic literacy

Curricula and instruction that respect diversity ensure that children have experience that "builds positive images, challenges young children's stereotypes, offers children tools for change, and addresses issues of exclusion and inclusion in age-appropriate contexts" (Hyson, 2004, p. 29). While engaged in this appropriate multicultural experience, you must be aware of how children respond emotionally to exclusion, bias, and difference, and plan for classroom activities and responses accordingly. Thus, as a teacher, you balance the individual's traditions as well as respect for all of the diversity represented in your classroom setting—ethnic, social class, gender—with an emphasis on social responsibility and the provision of opportunities for those who may experience discrimination in other social settings. In this way, the teacher is the key to breaking previously established barriers and traditions, that is, the preeminent role of dominant value orientation that may limit the respect for diversity.

## The "Common Good"

An important part of the social studies, even for young children, is an emphasis on social responsibility and civic engagement in a democratic society. Such focus ensures that young citizens learn to appreciate their responsibilities for citizenship. Thus, the curriculum must facilitate the development of attitudes, knowledge, and skills that will enable individuals to function in both their own communities and in those of others. This public school responsibility becomes ever more critical to think about as our schools become increasingly diverse. At a recent global conference, Banks (2004) stated that all children must see themselves in the citizenship education curriculum. For if they don't, then as adolescents and adults they will only be able to identify with

> the overarching national identity only to the extent that it mirrors their own perspectives, struggles, hopes, and possibilities. A curriculum that incorporates only the knowledge, values, experiences, and perspectives of mainstream powerful groups marginalizes the experiences of students who are members of racial, cultural, language, and religious minorities. Such a curriculum will not foster an overarching national identity because students will view it as one that has been created and constructed by outsiders, people who do not know, understand, or value their cultural and community experiences. (Banks, 2004, p. 13)

## Ethical Implications for Teachers in the Press for Accountability

Early childhood teachers and scholars have always placed a high value on meeting children where they are and helping them move forward. In our diverse society, this is ever more important. Teachers, thus, need to learn about the cultural traditions of the children they teach. There is a need to teach with respect for all children and parents and to bridge the gap for children who need more scaffolding. For the overall goal is that the social interactions at school that are based on sensitivity to children's social experiences elsewhere will help assure that children develop problem-solving skills, autonomy, self-esteem, and self-efficacy. Thus, children become resilient enough to handle the frustrations of ever-increasing academic demands in complicated classrooms.

An educator states, "the bottom line is that effective schools create instructional spaces where identity, intellect, and imagination are negotiated between teachers and students in ways that actively challenge coercive relations of power in the wider society" (Cummins, 2003, p. 58). Other educators support this view as follows: "[O]ur classroom was full of human knowledge. We had a teacher who believed in us; he didn't hide our power; he advertised it" (Jasso & Jasso, 1995, p. 255).

## Character Education

In reformulating "school" in the last decade and more, public debate converges on the civility of society—particularly as the norms are developed in the institution where children spend almost as much time as at home. Thus, as the social studies promote *the common good*, the debate about *character* becomes an integral part of the social studies curriculum—with the attendant focus on "good" and "right" behavior, grounded in moral precepts. The dicey part of this discussion comes about when "right" is juxtaposed with the goals of a pluralistic society. While there are "absolutes" that transcend culture, for example, most societies define *murder* as absolutely wrong, there are some exceptions made by certain societies that support "murder" if a "higher" moral (defined by the culture) principle can be applied. In the case of school and family issues, there are some not so clear customs that are culturally determined. For example, whose job is it to go to school to meet the teacher—the father, the mother, both parents? The answer varies.

The nexus of diversity across families and communities is critical in the lives of young children. Otherwise the effort to respect and support community risks encountering the dangers of schools of the recent past through a reemphasis on the *hidden curriculum* (Giroux, 1983). The hidden curriculum is one in which children were judged as "less worthy" or inadequate because of their ethnic, economic, social, and family status. The devastating consequences of this value set, pushed to the extreme, culminated in the President's Panel on Mental Retardation publication of the *Six-Hour Retarded Child* (1968). This panel documented schools where children found themselves treated to a less cognitively rigorous curriculum as a result of their failure at *school tasks* while in the community they functioned with aplomb and complexity.

The negatively applied hidden curriculum can be turned around when schools collaborate with the communities they serve in order to focus on the values of the community. A recent example in process is an effort of the Chicago Public Schools. The prime focus of Chicago community leaders and parents is on achievement and accountability with the attendant values of outcome-based education that assume hard work and responsibility for results on the part of all constituents—children, teachers, parents, and systemwide administrators.

> Schools avoid the trendy and are responsive to community need when the focus is on such stern virtues as persistence at hard tasks, courage in the face of difficulties, and patience ... recognition that character development and morality have deep religious roots ... that a clear recognition of the virtues required by the community must be understood by all ... and that teachers must regain moral authority in the lives of children. (Ryan & Bohlin, 1999)

Law and good practice already require that teachers serve as advocates for the young children in their care through such responsibilities as mandated reporting of child abuse. A key responsibility of teachers in the twenty-first century is participating in the definition, articulation, and advocacy of a set of virtues to provide the keys for academic mastery for all children.

Respect, responsibility, and self-discipline, the core values of character education (Ryan & Bohlin, 1999), begin in the early years for young people who later face choices that lead to participation in gang violence, precocious sexual activity, and substance abuse. Through the formal curriculum, these values are taught explicitly by the texts, stories, and other media chosen by teachers and children in the pursuit of understanding the themes. Through the hidden curriculum, children can "lose self-esteem, show unswerving obedience to silly rules, and suppress their individuality" (Ryan, 1995, p. 18).

Teachers can shift the hidden curriculum to ensure that "a spirit of fairness penetrates every corner of the school ... high standards teach habits of accuracy and precision ... self-control and self-discipline" (Ryan, 2001). In a practical way, teachers can focus on the six E's of character education—

> example, explanation, exhortation, ethos (or ethical environment), experience, and expectation of excellence.

These E's serve teachers as strategies for imparting the shared virtues and values of the community in smoothing the way for young children's school success (Mindes & Donovan, 2001, pp. 6–7).

In these ways, teachers show children fairness by modeling it, explaining the elements of honesty, asserting the importance of honor, setting up an environment that supports all learners, providing experiences for learning that rely on scaffolding, and expecting success for all learners.

This kind of education is "values attached to custom" (Cummings & Harlow, 2000, p. 306). To participate meaningfully in a democratic classroom where values are explored, children must be able to see the principle of cognitive reciprocity, an ability to see another's point of view, and exhibit mutual respect for others. "Moral education in a democracy, then, should stimulate and encourage reciprocity and mutual respect, and it is the school's responsibility to move children from heteronomy and unilateral respect to autonomy and mutual respect" (Cummings & Harlow, 2000, p. 306).

Moral values and a feeling of moral necessity is a constructive process elaborated as children are confronted with the needs and rights of others (DeVries et al., 2000, p. 11). Initially, children functioning from the egocentric cognitive perspective may not appreciate or understand the reason for the value and conform to classroom behavioral expectations out of obedience rather than out of conscience or the wish to do the right thing. As they mature, young children gradually learn empathy, and come to appreciate the community norms. This happens as teachers intentionally structure classroom experiences for children that will support their evolving social–emotional skills and provide the cognitive support to be able in years to come to articulate the reasons and values behind moral actions.

Lickona (2004, pp. 111–120) suggests practical principles for teachers to consider in the character education in the curriculum. These are as follows:

- relationships matter, so plan to relate individually to each child and to promote relationships among and between children

- bond through social convention such as "handshake," so use the conventions of social pleasantries to promote and receive respect
- know students as individuals with personalities, cultural perspectives, and cognitive approaches
- positive relationships with teachers influence child behavior, so think about it when you start with the negative in interactions with children
- teach by example with respect for students, as shown by personal interest in the stories they tell and the stresses they bring

Students can also be involved in identifying the "virtues" needed for school behavior. Often child involvement in identifying "virtues" occurs while reading children's literature and discussing the values implicit or explicit in the stories. For example, after reading *Will I Have a Friend?* (Cohen, 1989), children identify that kindness is a virtue in school relationships. Or when reading and discussing *Bears* (Kraus, 2005), children identify honesty as a virtue for everyday life. As well, children might identify the virtues of courage, courtesy, fairness, kindness, honesty, honor, justice, respect, responsibility, tolerance, and integrity. Through discussion and activities with students, these virtues can be given the appropriate developmental level. For example, courage for a kindergartener may mean speaking in a loud enough voice to be heard by the whole class.

In the curriculum, character education occurs through the choices that teachers select to illustrate "a primary source of our shared moral wisdom [through] stories, biographies, historical events, and ... reflections on the 'good life' and the meaning of 'strong moral character'" (Bohlin, Farmer, & Ryan, 2001, p. 39). Thus, the complexities and nuances of character education belong in the social studies, where the curriculum focuses on people in the broadest sense, such as culture, history, and human interactions with one another and with their environment. As an example, the often-repeated line "the policeman is your friend" as part of a community helpers study may not be true for some African American children (Walker & Snarey, 2004). The truth in character education and curriculum is more shaded and the stories or other curricular materials a teacher chooses to share with children should reflect these cultural nuances.

## Summary

This chapter addressed the evolving social self of a young child in relation to child care and school settings. The role of the center/school in this transformation is highlighted as well as the link to relationships with parents in the process. Classroom community, rules, social skills teaching, and character education are topics that link to this social development in young children. The role of social development to the content of social studies is made with an emphasis on the critical role of the valuable variety in culture and the shared human experiences across diverse cultures.

## Activities in the Field

1. Observe children of different ages (3–8) in a social situation—school, community center, park, home—how do they interact? What is the conversation? The gestures? How do they use space? How do they resolve conflict?

2. Interview a teacher to ask how she learns about the cultures of the children in each class. How does she adjust teaching to accommodate children? What role do parents play in the process?

3. Think back to your early school years, what was your school self and how did it evolve or change to the present moment?

## Activities in the Library

1. Begin an annotated list of children's books that you might use to teach social skills, character education, and community building.

2. Look at character education, historically, paying particular attention to the Progressive Era of the 1930s. How are the issues of today similar? Different?

## Study Questions

1. What role do teachers play in the development of a child's social self?

2. Where do rules fit into the curriculum? How do you establish these?

3. What is a hidden curriculum? How do you identify its characteristics?

4. When does character education become controversial? How do you prevent controversy? Or should you?

## Reflect and Re-read

1. How do children evolve socially?

2. How do families and schools work together for a smooth transition for young children?

3. Why is social learning and character education a part of the social studies?

## Suggested Readings

Barrera, I., & Corson, R. M. (2003). *Skilled dialogue: Strategies for responding to cultural diversity in early childhood*. Baltimore: Paul H. Brookes. Written for early childhood special educators, this book provides much practical guidance for relating to parents. In addition, the book has a description of many aspects of culture as this applies to children and families.

Kemple, K. M. (2004) *Let's be friends: Peer competence and social inclusion in early childhood programs*. New York: Teachers College Press. A book that gives suggestions for teacher intervention to facilitate inclusion of all children into a classroom's community.

Meisels, S. J., Marsden, D. B., & Stetson, C. (2000). *Winning ways to learn: 600 great ideas for children*. New York: Goddard Press. While written for parents as a resource to facilitate school success for young children three through five, the book describes specific ways to promote social behavior that may be useful for teachers as well.

Spring, J. (2004). *The intersection of cultures: Multicultural education in the United States and the global economy* (3rd ed.). New York: McGraw-Hill. This book is a thoughtful reflection with concrete suggestions for teachers from pedagogy of difference perspective.

### Children's Literature

Cohen, R. (1989). *Will I have a friend?* New York: Aladdin.
Henkes, K. (1996) *Chrysanthemum*. New York: Harper Torch.
Kraus, R. (2005). *Bears*. New York: HarperCollins.

## References

Angell, A. V. (2004). Making peace in elementary classrooms: A case for class meetings. *Theory and Research in Social Education, 32*(1), 98–104.

Banks, J. A. (Ed.). (2004). *Diversity and citizenship education: Global perspectives*. San Francisco: Jossey-Bass.

Berry, C. F., & Mindes, G. (1993). *Planning a theme-based curriculum: Goals, themes, activities and planning guides for 4's and 5's*. Glenview, IL: Good Year Books.

Bohlin, K. E., Farmer, D., & Ryan, K. (2001). *Building character in schools: A resource guide*. San Francisco: Jossey-Bass.

Brooks, N. (1879). Abe Lincoln's imagination. *Scribner's Monthly, 18*, 586.

Cummins, J. (2003). Challenging the construction of difference as deficit: Where are identity, intellect, imagination, and power in the new regime of truth. In P. P. Trifonas (Ed.), *Pedagogies of difference: Rethinking education for social change*. New York: Routledge Falmer.

Cummings, R., & Harlow, S. (2000, Summer). The constructivist roots of moral education. *Educational Forum, 64*, 300–307.

DeVries, R., Hildebrandt, C., & Zan, B. (2000). Constructivist early education for moral development. *Early Childhood Education Journal, 30*(1), 9–35.

Giroux, H. (1983). *Theory and resistance in education.* New York: Bergin & Garvey.

Hyson, M. (2004). *The emotional development of young children: Building an emotion-centered curriculum* (2nd ed.). New York: Teachers College Press.

Jasso, A., & Jasso, R. (1995). Critical pedagogy: Not a method, but a way of life. In J. Frederickson (Ed.), *Reclaiming our voices: Bilingual education, critical pedagogy & praxis* (pp. 253–259). Los Angeles: California Association for Bilingual Education.

Kemple, K. M. (2004). *Let's be friends: Peer competence and social inclusion in early childhood programs.* New York: Teachers College Press.

Killen, M., Ardila-Rey, A., & Barakkatz, M. (2000). Preschool teachers' perceptions about conflict resolution, autonomy, and the group in four countries: United States, Colombia, El Salvador, and Taiwan. *Early Childhood Education Journal, 30*(1), 73–92.

Knoff, H. (2001). *The Stop and Think Social Skills Program.* Longmont, CO: Sopris West.

Lickona, T. (2004). *Character education: How to help our children develop good judgment, integrity, and other essential virtues.* New York: Touchtone.

Mindes, G., & Donovan, M. A. (2001). *Building character: Five enduring themes for a stronger early childhood curriculum.* Needham Heights, MA: Allyn & Bacon.

President's Panel on Mental Retardation. (1968). *The six-hour retarded child.* Washington, DC: Author.

Ramirez, M., & Casteneda, A. (1974). *Cultural democracy, bicognitive development and education.* New York: Academic Press.

Ryan, K. (1995). Character first. *The American School Board Journal, 182*(6), 25–26.

Ryan, K. (2000). The six E's of character education. Retrieved from http://education.bu.edu/CharacterEd.

Ryan, K., & Bohlin, K. E. (1999). *Building character education in schools: Practical ways to bring moral instruction to life.* San Francisco: Jossey-Bass.

Singer, J. L. (1973). The child's world of make-believe. New York: Academic Press.

Stanulis, R. N., & Manning, B. H. The teacher's role in creating a positive verbal and nonverbal environment in the early childhood classroom. *Early Childhood Education Journal, 30*(1), 3–8.

Stone, J. G. (2001). *Building classroom community: The early childhood teacher's role.* Washington, DC: National Association for the Education of Young Children.

Upright, R. L. (2002). To tell a tale: The use of moral dilemmas to increase empathy in the elementary school child. *Early Childhood Education Journal, 30*(1), 15–20.

Vance, E., & Weaver, P. (2002). Class meetings: Young children solving problems together. *Young Exceptional Children, 11*, 2–9.

Walker, V. S., & Snarey, J. R. (2004). *Race-ing moral formation: African American perspectives on care and justice.* New York: Teachers College Press.

## Web Sites

Character Education Partnership: http://www.character.org. A group of nonpartisan organizations and individuals concerned with developing civic virtue in children and youth.

Civic Engagement Technical Assistance Center: http://www.cetac.org. This U.S. Department of Education Web site has the stated purpose for providing "technical assistance for implementing effective character education and civic engagement ... to serve as a resource for educators, parents, and the community at large."

## CHAPTER 3

# Teaching and Learning Social Studies in the Age of State Standards and Head Start Outcomes

Education . . . is a process of living and not a preparation for future living.

John Dewey (1897)

### Terms to Know

- Big ideas
- Theme-based content
- Scaffold
- School Self
- Common good
- Scope and sequence
- Integrated Curriculum
- Standards
- Big events
- Emergent literacy
- Functional language
- Expository text process skills
- High-stakes tests

### Overview

This chapter starts with the historical role of social studies in early childhood curricula. The discussion continues with a description of theme-based and problem-based organizational structures for the content of the social studies. Next is a featured review of position statements regarding the best ways to organize learning for young children. Examples of curricular topics that lead to the investigation of *big ideas* or important questions illustrate possibilities at both the preschool and the primary level. Finally, a focus on the "disappearance" of social studies from the primary curriculum is contrasted with a holistic way to incorporate reading instruction with social studies investigations.

## Focus Questions

1. What accomplishments do we expect young children to master through the content of social studies?
2. What are some effective ways to organize for mastery of the understandings and skills of social studies?
3. Which available position statements guide curricular decision making?
4. Using the position statements on planning curriculum, which important understandings are to be included and which topics lend themselves to significant investigations?
5. How does reading instruction support the teaching of social studies?
6. What do science and mathematics curricula offer to support the content of social studies?

## Historical Role of Social Studies in Early Childhood Education

Traditionally, an early childhood curriculum includes a central focus on social studies through content related to home and culture. In fact, one of the most prominent arguments for providing group play opportunities for young children comes from the idea that these experiences will help to socialize young children, that is, assist them in learning the ropes for engaging in the discourse of polite society, as well as facilitate their learning about the world (cf. Macmillan, 1930; Read & Patterson, 1980). This perspective is part of the broader "citizenship education" movement of social studies that began in the early part of the twentieth Century (Mindes, 2005, p. 12). Through the early play and preschool interactions, building on each child's home experiences, young children gain a greater awareness of school life and, ultimately, life in the community and beyond that creates the foundation of social studies. The social studies incorporate anthropology, economics, geography, political science, history, sociology, and psychology. From its inception, instruction in social studies content placed emphasis on the principles of democratic citizenship and the U.S. heritage, utilizing the many social sciences disciplines. As well, the initial and continued basic approach to social studies content development is an inquiry-based approach (Mindes, 2005).

Therefore, the social studies offer a structure for broad *theme-based content*—content organized around a topic that offers multiple entry points and significant opportunities for investigation. Theme-based experiences become a training ground for students to acquire problem-solving skills, as well as provide a laboratory for the development and elaboration of interpersonal coping skills and strategies. "The primary purpose of social studies is to help young people develop the ability to make informed and reasoned decisions for the public good as citizens of a culturally diverse, democratic society in an interdependent world" (National Council for the Social Studies [NCSS], 1994, p. 3).

## Organizing the Study of Social Studies from Themes and Problems

Often then, enduring life themes—family, school, and community—anchor the social studies content focus throughout the early childhood years. That is, as teachers you draw the "big ideas" about these topics to choose content in the familiar and to *scaffold*—make connections effectively—to new learning experiences about the world known and unknown to young children. For example, a study of family at the preschool and again at the primary level can help young children understand the many definitions of family as well as involve a group of children in the celebration of diverse cultural aspects of family life. Through story reading, science experiments, and mathematical investigations that pertain to family—for example, reading *The Relatives Came* (Rylant, 1985) about an extended family's visit, then analyzing the content of the crackers the relatives brought, and measuring the shoe sizes of everyone and creating a graph of the children's shoes and one for the adults'—sociological/anthropological understandings of family begin, in addition to literacy, scientific problem solving, and mathematical investigation. To continue to elaborate children's understanding of the world, school is often a topic of study as well as a place for the development of basic political understandings through the development of rules to govern group living.

## Activities to Facilitate Children's Understanding of the World and Its Structure

Thus, social studies are the activities that facilitate the building of classroom community and "school self," or the persona that evolves as a learner and member of the learning community. These activities are the classroom rule-making exercises, conflict resolution approaches, self-efficacy insights, and the concepts about group life—the ebb and flow of individual rights, such as the *common good* (the rights of the society) and the ultimate smooth functioning of a classroom of children from diverse backgrounds.

Therefore, given this rich inquiry-based history for the incorporation of social studies into the fabric of the early childhood curriculum, it is ironic that teachers report today, "There is no time for social studies in the curriculum." Where does the no-time argument come from? How does it fit with the best practice advocated by various professional organizations?

## Best Practice as Described by National Learned Societies

In its position statement "Developmentally Appropriate Practice in Early Childhood Programs Serving Children Birth to 8," the National Association for the Education of Young Children (NAEYC) includes many references to the historical and current relevance of social studies in the early childhood program (Bredekamp & Copple, 1997). These references include items like the importance of

- creating a caring environment,
- recognizing that children are best understood in the context of family, culture, and society,
- facilitating conceptual understanding in the primary years across all curricular domains,
- understanding that children learn through active engagement with the intellectually stimulating environment,
- providing a social context that supports learning,
- facilitating the development of responsibility and self-regulation on the part of children,
- constructing curricula with intellectual integrity, and
- establishing reciprocal relationships with families.

When reviewing these principles and others articulated in the position statement, it is easy to see that early childhood curricula must indeed be rich in the social studies.

The Division on Early Childhood (DEC) of the Council for Exceptional Children (CEC) is also a frequent co-signer of NAEYC position statements on appropriate practice in early childhood, including the principles outlined above. In addition, in *Recommended Practices* (Sandoval, McLean, & Smith, 2000) there is an emphasis on the importance of family and educator collaboration. This collaboration can improve the development and learning outcomes for young children with disabilities. In particular, the DEC *Recommended Practices* (Sandoval et al., 2000) addresses ways to improve social competence, independence, problem solving, and enhanced family functioning—all aspects of the social studies curricula.

As well, in a position statement on curricular standards, the National Association for Multicultural Education (NAME, 2001) highlights five key concerns about curriculum:

1. Inclusiveness of all peoples of the United States and the reciprocal relationships among diverse groups within our nation

2. Diverse perspectives for the historical, social, and natural phenomena included in curricular content

3. Provision of multiple paradigms for the construction and understanding of knowledge

4. Fostering a dynamic development of self-identity that includes the multiple and sometimes opposing realities of experience

5. Commitment to social justice that involves action on the part of learners and a critical understanding of diverse perspectives

Consequently, upon review of these position statements, teachers know that they must

- assist children in social–emotional growth,
- avoid an overemphasis on the "holiday" curriculum,
- seek an antibias approach to values,
- collaborate with parents, and
- foster the development of integrity in individuals and groups of children,

while teaching them all to read, write, compute, and problem-solve.
Through the social studies, then, socialization of young children to school
and society occurs while enabling the development of individuality and
independence.

For preschool and primary-aged children, the social studies serve an
especially important function. These are the critical years, when the tone
is set for each child's and family's interface with the system of school. Will
the school be a pleasant place where learning risks may be taken? Will the
school and teachers respect the child's culture and heritage? Will a cooperative community of learners be developed? Will students be supported
in the development of self-esteem as well as a *school character*? Thus, it is
through the content of social studies as defined by the NCSS that the social understandings are developed and respected. The NCSS Curriculum
Strands (NCSS, 1998) draw content from the following themes:

culture;

time, continuity, and change;

people, places, and environment;

individual development and identity;

individuals, groups, and institutions;

power, authority, and governance;

production, distribution, and consumption;

science, technology, and society;

global connections; and

civic ideals and practice.

The broad themes are incorporated through guided discovery in a
democratic classroom organized around "big ideas" emphasizing a developmentally continuous approach with an articulated *scope and sequence*—
defining the specific topics of instruction and the timeline for teaching
them. In this way, children develop a sense of self, problem-solving skills
as well as good citizenship traits. An *integrated curriculum* implies that
the traditional discrete subjects of "school" are organized around child-
friendly chunks that carry adult-important ideas. These are the ideas for-
mulated in the *standards* or statements of important learning accomplishments for all learners that are established by professional associations and
state, city, and suburban school systems. The themes allow young children the opportunity to use their budding academic skills of reading,

writing, and computing. In addition, children can pursue individual interests through the broad nature of the inquiry process that is central to theme development. Theme- and project-based teaching lends itself to activities that focus on small groups as well as individuals with intermittent large-group summarization and culmination projects. Thus, the process approximates the "real world" of problem solving, goal setting, and independence of effort.

## Effective Themes

To work effectively, themes must be those that reflect enduring and significant topics. In the early childhood years, these include social studies activities that address self, family, school, community, and the world of work, among others. The scope and sequence for the social studies in elementary school defined by the NCSS (1984, pp. 376–385) is as follows:

Kindergarten—awareness of self in social setting

First grade—the individual in school and family life

Second grade—the neighborhood

Third grade—sharing the earth with others in the community

Such themes are broad enough to offer the capacity to engage children's interests and talents at many levels. The activities drawn from these themes can change to meet current times. Furthermore, such themes offer real links to the social studies standards—a nationally agreed-upon target. Themes and activities connect to the national, state, and local learning standards for young children so they learn history, geography, economics, political science, anthropology, and sociology through the durable themes that connect to their lives—today, yesterday, and tomorrow.

Contrast these open-ended and abiding themes with those ever-popular and adult-led units of *blue week* or *dinosaur study* for two- and three-year-olds. How many children really need to spend a whole week concentrating on learning "blue"? What do they know after the experience? Will they function as color-coordinated adults? Does this advance the *common good*? Does it enhance their problem-solving abilities? And of what significance is a detailed study of dinosaurs to the children of the twenty-first century? Often, months of experiences with such topic involve quasi-scientific activities with a dubiously historic perspective for preschool and kindergarten children whose sense of time, particularly in relation to the past (last week, last year), is limited and evolving. The likes of blue week and dinosaur study themes come from the adult definition of learning needs for children and pay no attention to individual differences or curricular scope and sequence. They ultimately trivialize the learning process. Yes, it is conventional for children to recognize, label, and identify blue. Some children come to child care and educational settings knowing the concept. Why should they spend time perseverating on it? Dinosaur themes are found at every age level and in every guise for young children's consumption. To what end is this fascination contributing? Do young children require weeks and months of instruction on the topic? A more appropriate approach to the planning of curriculum pays attention to child construction of knowledge, skills, attitudes, and dispositions. Alleman and Brophy (2001, 2002, 2003) show the meaningful development of the themes of food, clothing, shelter, communication, transportation, family living, childhood, money, and government. For example, in the theme on childhood, children investigate cultural universals and differences, growth from babyhood to childhood, birthdays, rites of passage, child workers, schools, toys and entertainment, and children who make a difference (Alleman & Brophy, 2003, pp. 29–122). Each of these topics has multiple entry points, offers opportunities to link curricula across subject areas, and is inherently interesting to children.

In today's time, Operation Backpack began as charitable giving by children to the victims of Hurricane Katrina. The activity as part of a theme on Children Making a Difference provides discussion opportunities: What is a hurricane? What is the effect of hurricanes on a location? How do we help others in time of need? What are we willing to sacrifice from our possessions to help others? How will we collect and ship the backpacks? What should go in them? Why is the backpack an important symbol for children? These and other questions/activities not only serve the content purpose of social studies but also illustrate citizenship action. Of course, mathematics, geography, and reading activities are integral to the development and evolution of this course of study.

## Grounding for the Theme/Problem-Based Curricula

Such a philosophy of curriculum construction comes from the principles described by the NAEYC (Bredekamp & Copple, 1997, pp. 20–21), with the following guidelines for practice:

- attention to all areas of child development—physical, social–emotional, linguistic, aesthetic, and cognitive;

- provision of a broad range of content across traditional disciplines in a socially relevant, intellectually stimulating, and personally meaningful way;

- mindfulness of each child's knowledge base with provisions to build further upon the diverse conceptual frameworks of the children served;

- utilization of the cross-disciplinary approach to curriculum while providing opportunities for subject-matter focus;

- focus on processes and skills as well as dispositions and application strategies;

- employment of the principles of intellectual integrity for the choice of themes and activities;

- provision of support for the home community of each child as well as provision of opportunities for access and success in the larger community;

- regard for the realistic attainment of goals by children within a developmental range; and

- judicious incorporation of technology in support of the construction of knowledge by children.

The NAEYC principles are an agreed-upon body of wisdom that reflects best practice in the service of teaching and learning for young children.

While curriculum integration promotes access and understanding for young children, you will need to incorporate separate subjects in the overall curricular plan. This supports child investigation, vocabulary development, and the study of problems and issues that occur within the themes. The trick is that you must have goals for the learning activities tied to the theme, because children are most likely to show interest and learn when the curriculum is functional and meaningful to their backgrounds and experiences. The suitable early childhood classroom takes the demands of standards, plus the interests of children, and combines these to integrate the tasks of learning around significant themes that facilitate child understanding of subject matter, as well as individual concepts and constructs. These classrooms provide opportunities for individuals as well as the community of learners. Thus, the curriculum balances the whole and the individual in service to all.

So, you select a "big idea" to explore such as, Who lives in my community? Then, you organize activities and the environment to support the theme, choosing neighborhood pictures for the bulletin board and age/grade-appropriate activities for each of the learning centers—maps and timelines in the math center; books about community in the literacy center; blocks of various sizes in the science center for the construction of buildings; and charts and stories that children collect about the community displayed in the writing center. Once the room is set up for the children, they add to the environment as they explore the theme with artifacts displaying individual and group projects.

Such classrooms operate with an interplay of self-selected choice activities skillfully arranged at learning centers and/or large- and small-group activities that promote child-initiated choice and interaction with the classroom environment—materials, peers, and teacher. You orchestrate periods to support concentration, a flow from activity to activity, balance between types of activities, and recognition of the maturity level and previous social experiences of the particular young children involved. This classroom structure supports a social studies curriculum that is problem-based and thematically oriented.

In the social studies, children also need multiple opportunities to investigate significant questions across themes, to represent their learning through projects and to reflect on their learning through a portfolio or other assessment (Bickart, Jablon, & Dodge, 1999). Being based upon the set of values that embody the profession of early childhood and its definition of best practice, this approach to curricular practice is active and engaging.

Accordingly, by definition, theme-based curriculum planning promotes the integration of learning. Themes are broad and provide many entry points (See Table 3.1 for suggested themes and entry points.) for diverse learners to solve problems and to enhance personal understandings. Teachers incorporate ways to document the outcomes required by the community and the state when they construct the themes. Children have opportunities to demonstrate mastery through the products and processes in which they participate. Teachers structure and teach within the theme so that the stakeholder goals are met while each child, on the basis of personal interests, soars beyond minimalist standards.

## Teacher's Role in This Curricular Approach

Thus, the teacher's role is to promote discovery, suggest next steps, set the stage, facilitate, model, trust, accept child mistakes, treat children with dignity, instruct, manage, observe, evaluate, reflect, and plan. It is no small

**Table 3.1**
**Theme and Entry Points**

| Theme | Entry Points |
|---|---|
| Self | Drawing self-portrait |
| | Reading books all about me |
| | Tracing self in big outline on floor |
| | Measuring shoes of several classmates |
| | Developing timeline of life events |
| Family | Drawing pictures of family |
| | Reading books about families |
| | Making a family tree, including grandparents |
| | Surfing the Internet for information about families around the world |
| Community | Describing the neighborhood in words or pictures |
| | Collecting oral histories from long-time residents |
| | Making a map of the community |
| | Developing historical timeline for the community |
| State | Locating major cities on the map |
| | Visiting the Internet to collect information about seal, flag, motto, bird, or other symbol, of state |
| | Organizing graph to show population of state |
| | Graphing the economic products of the state |
| | Developing a tourist brochure |
| Bread | Reading stories about bread |
| | Taking a trip to the grocery store to see different kinds of bread |
| | Charting the kinds of bread that the class eats |
| | Making bread with yeast, making bread with baking soda/powder, making bread without leavening; compare process and results |
| Travel | Charting the ways children come to school. |
| | Charting the ways that families go to work. |
| | Reading stories about transportation. |
| | Examining public transportation routes for the community. |
| | Writing a position paper about transportation needs. |
| | Envisioning transportation in the future without oil. |

undertaking and not to be attempted by the faint-hearted. This role requires content knowledge along with regular reflection upon practice plus flexibility and creativity. The rewards are many, including the creation of a climate for successful learning and curricular mastery for all children.

Thematic integration of content promotes student learning. The theme, for example "pioneers," permits multiple entry points for each child. That is, each student can enter the pioneer theme activities with personal background of experiences and knowledge of family and community history. Thematic activities based on this theme might include small-group investigations focusing on travel, food, clothing, toys, etc. and thus have multiple outcomes that integrate discrete skills into a coherent whole. Such activities include foundations and extensions for literacy, numeracy, critical thinking, and cooperative learning. Such broad-based themes provide stimuli for activities that touch all the learning domains. Thus, teachers can reinforce concepts within and across domains as children learn new concepts. Opportunities for expanding the themes in order to elaborate or to develop further understanding in individual children or in the group must be a part of the ongoing planning and assessment that accompanies theme-based teaching.

In addition to promoting integration of learning, themes offer opportunities for creating the "big events" in the community of the classroom. The big events are an outgrowth or culmination of a theme or parent events, assembly performances, classroom newspaper, or other major enterprises that may emerge or be planned. Typical products of learning in this kind of teaching are the drawing and writing that children do to share with their peers, teachers, and parents. Processes that foster the investigative skills of children are the use of reading and discussion in pursuit of problem solution. The themes can emerge through a study of problems determined by the teacher and children in pursuit of understanding the social studies standards. The problems studied can be as simple as care for teeth during the dental health month. Besides the science and health aspects applied to the topic, young children can investigate historical and technological advancement in the care of teeth as well as the influence of teeth decay on total body health—including a bit of sociology regarding access to health care.

## Practical Examples of Curricular Implementation at the Preschool and Primary Level

More elaborate examples of thematic and problem-based units of study include the following example found in typical preschool curricula, such as transportation—How do we go from here to there and where are we going? Where have we been? Through investigation, young children develop a sense of the kinds of transportation available to their families and community. The investigatory methods might include observing modes of transportation during field trips, reading books about travel, viewing videos about travel, making charts that show the ways families go to work, making graphs that show how they get to school, making charts that illustrate family vacations or celebrations and how they got there. They may learn about ways that their grandparents traveled by conducting interviews. The investigation can include rudimentary map making and books made to represent family and/or class trips. Young children may also be curious about fuel costs, since the topic is often a daily part of the evening news. Thus, their curiosity may lead them to investigations of where gas comes from? How is price determined? There can be debates about public transportation versus individual car/truck movement. Through such activities that are appropriately scaled for young children's investigation, they are learning how to state hypotheses and how to gather evidence. They also are developing a rudimentary knowledge of economics. As well, the tenet of the "common good" and other democratic principles may be a part of the discussion.

In another preschool, children may be investigating plants and animals in their community. The investigation may begin with a discussion about the plants or animals in the classroom. Then, study can expand to include the home, with children describing plants and animals there. The kinds of plants or animals can be charted. Of course, books about plants and animals in the region will expand knowledge, for example, desert plants and animals for those living in Phoenix. On the one hand, the content for this theme-based investigation will depend upon whether the children live in a rural area that includes animals and plants as part of the economic fiber of the community. On the other hand, they may live in suburbia, with lawns and gardens, or in the inner city, which may contain community gardens, zoos, and large amounts of concrete. Nevertheless, through this preschool community-specific investigation, young children will be discovering the interrelationships of plants and animals with their families and child care centers in a real-world context.

At the primary level, immigration is a theme that is potentially rich with multicultural understanding. The content for this theme will depend upon the community and the heritage of the children. However, it is easy to imagine that children in our transient society with long-standing roots to the community can engage in the theme through investigation into the personal histories of their extended families. While moving from Texas to Montana may not be an immigration experience, young children can apply the investigation to such long-distance moves that they may have experienced. Finally, besides the obvious geography skills that children will apply, they will have opportunities to investigate a rich literature about their personal heritage and those of others through children's literature that is widely available on the topic. There are children's books by several authors that you might choose, depending on your focus and your communities, for example, those by Wolf (2003), Anzaldua (1993), Bial (2002), and Collier (1999). (See Children's Literature below.)

Two other examples of themes that offer multidimensional study include ecology and money. While often considered a "science" topic, ecology offers much for investigation regarding land and land use, conservation of energy, and resources for the public good. The topic of money involves not only the recognition of currency and the computation of currency amounts, but also the rich themes of trade, shopping, saving, budgeting, and economic resource comparisons across the city, state, or country. In each of the investigations that you and your children may conduct on these or other broad-based problems that offer opportunities for young children to investigate "big ideas," you have the opportunity not only to embed scientific principles of investigation and data collection, but also to use diverse children's literature sources collected from the library, children's newspapers, and the Internet. In this way, you are building on children's *emergent literacy*, which is described with the following characteristics:

- Children begin to read and write very early in life by recognizing trademarks and other familiar words as well as by drawing and using letters as symbols and invented spelling.
- Children learn the functions of literacy by participating in real-life reading and writing activities.
- Reading and writing begin in tandem through experiences with books, reading, and various writing and drawing materials.
- As young children read, listen, write, and draw, they develop an understanding of literacy. (Teale & Sulzby, 1989)

Therefore, in the social studies, children's literature, maps, atlases, the Internet, and all the tools of the social scientists serve to promote the development of literacy and the acquisition of knowledge, skills, and attitudes that promote social understandings.

## The Disappearance of Social Studies
## Content in Favor of Reading

Thus, it is ironic that time in the day for social studies is often grabbed for reading, when, through the application of an emergent literacy philosophy, you can nurture the integration of the thematic curriculum. Early childhood teachers know that children are "natural" language users and bring many language skills to their first formal education settings. Young students thrive in environments where they enjoy numerous and varied opportunities to use and develop all the four language processes—speaking, listening, reading, and writing. These processes are taught and modeled across the curriculum—in scientific thinking, mathematical reasoning, the arts, social studies, and so forth—so that children will grow in their ability to formulate and express their ideas. Teachers choose social studies themes to meet young children's need for understanding themselves and the world around them. They start with narratives—stories—during sharing time and expand students' understandings with books. This way, children's home literacy experiences are validated first, then enlarged with exposure to the language and workings of school.

For example, children choose print media with the guidance of teachers and parents to answer their curiosity about the concept of *family*. They learn about their own families through the study of pictures and photographs as well as the oral histories and stories they gather from parents, siblings, and relatives. They learn about other families (and build skills in comparing and contrasting) through picture books, folk tales, and real-life adventure stories as well as newspapers and magazines. Further development of reading skills and dispositions—as well as concepts of family—comes with judicious exposure to thematically related computer software, videos, and other tools of a literate society. Examples of software include KidPix® 4 (http://riverdeep.net); TimeLiner v 5.0, Tom Snyder/Scholastic (http://tomsnyder.com); and Eyewitness Children's Encyclopedia (http://riverdeep.net).

As children mature, their mastery of *functional language*, that is, the language of everyday life and increasingly the language of "school"—the vocabulary and expressions used specifically to learn—develops through the use of writing and speaking skills to confirm new knowledge. Examples of functional language are terms such as table of contents, map, globe, encyclopedia, etc. and *expository text-processing skills*, such as description, sequence, comparison, cause and effect; problem and solution (cf. Tompkins, 2006). Such expositions would include picture drawing, story mapping, charting, graphing, e-mailing, and personal dictionaries.

**Figure 3.1**
**Cause and Effect Diagram**

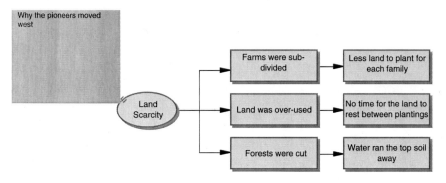

Through the excitement generated by a thematic study, children demonstrate their mastery via the products of their investigations.

Additional potential products appropriate to the themes of social studies include the production of plays, art shows, and other examples of cooperative learning. Through the literacy experiences attached to thematic social studies (see Figures 3.1 and 3.2.), children learn that these subjects, skills, and dispositions are suited to the exploration and development of social and personal knowledge. What remains, then, is the capacity to show the gains to the stakeholders—parents, principal, and others.

Such an approach to reading instruction is in contrast to the "drill and practice" version of teaching reading alone for 60 minutes per day found around the country in school districts that are concerned with improving performance on *high-stakes tests*—single measures that have life consequences for individuals or schools. In these districts, often teachers are required to use materials for instruction that focus on skills rather than the application of skills. These approaches, the belief goes, will improve performance on tests. Thus, young children spend much of their day engaged in curriculum that is devoid of consideration of "big ideas." Instead, the focus is test-prep. Also, since the scores must be good at the end of the day, the number of minutes specified for reading (and mathematics) instruction absorbs the better part of the day and social studies instruction drops to the bottom of the priority for the early childhood curriculum. Therefore, you will need to be a skillful teacher who can incorporate the "big ideas" of social studies into the reading program for your students. This can happen through your choice of reading materials that include opportunities for young children to investigate problems of interest to

**Figure 3.2
Story Map**

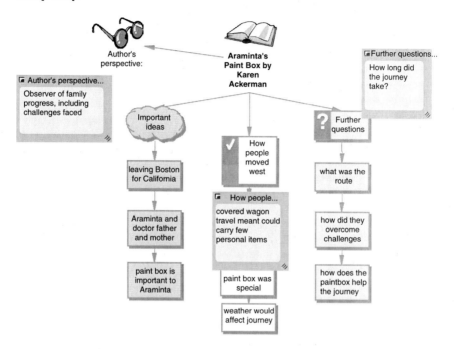

them that also foster learning in geography, history, economics, political science, anthropology, and sociology. Such reading activities will include map reading, landform analysis, community historical continuity, as well as relevant state history—trade relations, exchange of goods and services, elections, and how people interact today, or did in the past, and around the world to celebrate, as well as live, their daily lives. Map reading can begin with the construction of a class map, and then proceed to the interpretation of a city or county map. Models of mountains and valleys as well as plains can be constructed with sand and clay. Community history can be described by the historical society representative who brings artifacts and pamphlets depicting local history. Newspapers can be used to review topics related to trade. All of these activities of course depend on the age and stage of the learners involved. Example lesson plans and lists of appropriate books are available on the following Web sites: Carol Hurst's children's literature site, http://www.carolhurst.com; MarcoPolo, Social Studies and Language Arts Integrated, http://www.marcopolo-education.org; ReadWriteThink, Standards Based Teaching, http://www.readwritethink.org.

## Managing the Scarcity of Time in the Day/Year of a Child

This integrated approach to teaching requires that you carefully guard the use of time—looking at the significant and important rather than the trivial as you choose whether to spend two weeks on a theme related to a study of Cinderella around the world. By contrast, you may choose to spend two weeks examining the implications of drilling for oil in the wildlife sanctuary of Alaska. While both investigations may fully engage, the interests of children and many cultural understandings come from the study of folk myths around the world, particularly those involving a common theme; you will need to decide and justify, especially to yourself, the choices that you make. In making the choices for supporting students' interests as they investigate a particular topic, look back to the state standards that you are required to include in the curricula. How will you address the standards in the problem-based investigation? What reading, language arts, and mathematical skills and aptitudes do children advance? How will you ensure that young children progress in the development of critical analyses? How will you assess the progress they make in comparison with the standards? As you think through these and other practical aspects of teaching, you will make the choices that prepare young children for success on high-stakes measures, as well as engage them in the understandings that enable them to move about effectively in their social world today and tomorrow.

## Summary

This chapter began with a review of the historical role of social studies in early childhood curricula. The discussion continued with a description and illustrations of theme- and problem-based planning. Next, the position statements of appropriate curriculum guides link planning decisions with examples for possible classroom use. A particular concentration on linking reading instruction to social studies planning shows how social studies fits the busy school calendar, especially at the primary level.

## Activities in the Field

1. Visit a preschool and a primary class. Identify the implicit and explicit examples of socials studies content.
2. Interview an experienced teacher who uses problem-based learning. How does the teacher meet the demands for accountability while planning investigative curricula with the children?

## Activities in the Library

1. Go to the Library of Congress Web site http://www.loc.gov. Examine the materials available for teachers and "kids and families." How might you use these to meet the social studies standards for a particular grade in your state?

2. Examine reading, math, and social studies child textbooks for a particular grade. How might you use these resources in a series of problem-based units?

## Study Questions

1. What are the historical underpinnings for social studies education?

2. What does the theme- or problem-based approach to curricular planning contribute to the effective development of social studies lessons?

3. How do the position statements of professional associations contribute to the articulation of your social studies teaching philosophy?

4. How does the emergent literacy philosophy contribute to the integration of reading and social studies instruction?

5. In what ways can you integrate math and science with social studies?

6. What are some important considerations when choosing among possible themes to study with the children?

## Reflect and Re-read

1. Why do some teachers say that social studies content is the foundational platform for all other curricula in early childhood?

2. What argument can you make that supports the integration of reading and social studies even at times of high-stakes accountability?

## Suggested Readings

Alleman, J., & Brophy, J. (2003). *Social studies excursions, K-3. Books 1-3*. Portsmouth, NH: Heinemann. Practical examples of lessons that incorporate the "big ideas" of social studies.

Frost, J. L., Wortham, S. C., & Reifel, S. (2005). *Play and child development* (2nd ed.). Upper Saddle River, NJ: Merrill. In this book, the authors review the history of play, describe what it looks like at various ages, and show how play is linked to the curriculum.

Lambros, A. (2002). *Problem-based learning in K-8 classrooms: A teacher's guide to implementation.* Thousand Oaks, CA: Corwin. The author defines problem-based learning and gives practical examples for using the technique.

Seefeldt, C. (2005). *How to work with standards in the early childhood classroom.* A practical application for the challenges that teachers face in high-stakes accountability situations. New York: Teachers College.

## References

Alleman, J., & Brophy, J. (2001). *Social studies excursions K-3, Book one: Powerful units on food, clothing, and shelter.* Portsmouth, NH: Heinemann.

Alleman, J., & Brophy, J. (2002). *Social studies excursions K-3, Book two: Powerful units on communication, transportation and family living.* Portsmouth, NH: Heinemann.

Alleman, J., & Brophy, J. (2003). *Social studies excursions K-3, Book three: Powerful units on childhood, money, and government.* Portsmouth, NH: Heinemann.

Archambault, R. D. (Ed.). (1964). *John Dewey on education–Selected writings* (p. 430). New York: Random House.

Bickart, T. S., Jablon, J. R, & Dodge, D. T. (1999). *Building the Primary Classroom: A Complete Guide to Teaching and Learning.* Washington, DC: Teaching Strategies, Inc.

Bredekamp, S., and Copple, C. (Eds.). (1997). *Developmentally appropriate practice in early childhood programs* (rev. ed.). Washington, DC: National Association for the Education of Young Children.

Dewey, J. (1897, January 16). My pedagogic creed. *The School Journal, LIV*(3), 77–80.

Macmillan, M. (1930). *The nursery school.* New York: E.P. Dutton.

Mindes, G. (2005). Social studies in today's early childhood curricula. *Young Children, 60*(5), 12–18.

National Association for Multicultural Education. (2001). *Criteria for evaluating state curriculum standards.* Washington, DC: Author.

National Council for Social Studies. (1994). *Curriculum standards for social studies expectations of excellence.* Washington, DC: Author.

Read, K., & Patterson, J. (1980). *The nursery school and kindergarten: Human relationships and learning* (7th ed.). New York: Holt, Rinehart and Winston.

Sandoval, S., McLean, M. E., & Smith, B. J. (Eds.). (2000). *DEC recommended practices in early intervention/early childhood special education.* Missoula, MT: Division on Early Childhood.

Teale, W. H., & Sulzby, E. (1989). Emerging literacy: New perspectives. In D. S. Strickland & L. M. Morrow (Eds.), *Emerging literacy: Young children learn to read and write* (pp. 1–15). Newark, DE: International Reading Association.

Tompkins, G. E. (2006). *Literacy for the 21st century: A balanced approach* (4th ed.). Upper Saddle River, NJ: Merrill/Prentice Hall.

### Children's Literature

Ackerman, K. (1998). *Araminta's paintbox.* B. Lewin (Illus.). New York: Aladin.

Anzaldua, G. (1993). *Friends from the other side/Amigos del Otro Lado.* C. Mendez (Illus.). San Francisco: Children's Book Press.

Bial, R. (2002). *Tenement: Immigrant life on the Lower East Side.* Boston: Houghton Mifflin.

Collier, C. (1999). *A century of immigration: 1820–1924.* New York: Marshall Cavendish/Benchmark Books.

Rylant, C. (1985). *The relatives came.* New York: Simon & Schuster.

Wolf, B. (2003). *Coming to America: A Muslim family's story.* New York: Lee & Low.

## *Web Sites*

Division on Early Childhood: http://www.dec-sped.org. This site contains information about publications related to early childhood special education.

National Association for the Education of Young Children: http://www.naeyc. org. This site shows position papers and practical examples for teaching.

National Association for Multicultural Education: http://nameorg.org. This site contains position statements and practical information for teaching.

## CHAPTER 4

# The Context of Culture in Teaching Social Studies: Beyond the Antibias Curriculum

Leslie R. Williams and Gayle Mindes

If we are to achieve a richer culture, rich in contrasting values, we must recognize the whole gamut of human potentialities, and so weave a less arbitrary social fabric, one in which each diverse human gift will find a fitting place. Margaret Mead (1935)

## Terms to Know

- Culture
- Context
- Multicultural Perspectives
- Multicultural Approaches
- Antibias Curriculum
- Social Justice
- Global Education

## Overview

As you continue to think about teaching social studies to young children, pause now to think more deeply about why there are so many reminders in the text about the recognition of culture as a crucial aspect of your work as a teacher of early childhood social studies. Before deciding that *culture* and perhaps *multicultural approaches* to curriculum and teaching are overused terms, consider that the very essence of child and family in a social context always includes the cultural interpretation of family by those who are significant persons in all children's lives. When thinking about *young* children, whose lives are still closely tied to the immediate worlds of their families, respect for and understanding of cultures and cultural differences are critical. The concepts apply to all families. Our thinking through the issues of culture, thus, should not be considered relevant only when working with children and families who are recent immigrants to the community from a distant land and who speak a language other than English at home.

What is clear to most teachers grappling with the concept of culture is that the term has several meanings according to the aspect of this complex phenomenon that is being emphasized at the moment. Culture is especially important for those of us working with young children, because culture *is* the moment-to-moment enactments of their daily lives, within their families, their schools, and their communities. And culture is part of the inheritance of every human being, regardless of where they are now living, or may have come from previously, or what language they may speak (De Gaetano, Williams, & Volk, 1998). Culture has been thought to be a unique human creation[1]; it is not something that children are born with, but something that they acquire through interaction with families and others in the community. Being a human creation, culture changes constantly over time, from generation to generation, and from location to location, according to the social experiences of those involved. Culture is part of who you are as adult teachers, as much as it is part of the children and families that you will serve. Thus, culture is everywhere, affecting all of us all of the time, and, being so pervasive, it must be recognized, integrated, and acknowledged in order for your teaching and learning to have lasting meaning (De Gaetano et al., 1998).

Because of this pervasive quality, culture is the prime context for teaching not only social studies, but also for teaching any subject. It is a common misconception that multicultural approaches to teaching and learning really need to be considered only in the area of social studies, but in fact it is just as important—if not more so by its frequent absence—to integrate multicultural perspectives into, for example, the teaching of science and mathematics to appreciate that these areas too represent varying views of "reality." As this text is devoted to the teaching of social studies, however, the exploration of the relevance of culture is left to this area alone. First is a review of definitions of culture and the meanings of contexts in early educational settings. Then comes an examination of the appearance of culture in the physical settings of classrooms; interactions with children, families, and other teachers; and the content of social studies learning activities. Finally, look at ways that you as teachers, through multicultural awareness, may expand—not inhibit—the growth of students as citizens of the world and document your work and children's learning through assessment activities.

## Focus Questions

1. What is culture, and how does it play out in the lives of young children?

2. In what ways does culture mediate between children's social development and the content of social studies?

3. What are common multicultural approaches to the teaching of social studies, and what are the multicultural perspectives that they are drawing upon?

4. How do multicultural approaches to teaching social studies fit with the use of state standards and Head Start outcomes?

5. What is the relationship of multicultural approaches to teaching social studies, antibias curriculum, teaching for social justice, and global education for young children?

6. What is the role of multicultural perspectives in teaching social studies and the assessment of children's achievement?

## Culture, Context, and Meaning

In the opening chapter of this text, there are several definitions of *culture*. Through this varied array, the intent is to illuminate the complexity of the concept and the far-ranging area that it influences. The introduction also prepared the way for the deeper discussion of the relationships between the specifics of culture, educational contexts, and the making of meaning that follows. In all of the definitions examined, it seemed that there were three major domains that provide evidence of culture. These are

1. the domain of material artifacts (such as the products of architecture, art, and music; the artifacts of religion or home making, or tools for interaction with the environment; and the choice of foods eaten, locations lived in, or materials used in educational settings),

2. the domain of behaviors (such as the ways that families and communities take care of young children, the ways that individuals move

through space, the ways that families and societies communicate with others, or the ways that families and communities celebrate special events in the family), and

3. the domain of ideas, the thoughts (such as values, belief systems, and worldviews) about self in relation to the rest of the world and the cosmos.

These three domains are identified by some multicultural early educators as the *what*, the *how*, and the *why* of cultures (Williams, De Gaetano, Harrington, & Sutherland, 1985).

It is not uncommon for early educators who are interested in integrating multicultural perspectives into their social studies curriculum to focus on the first domain—the materials that stem from particular cultures—and make diversity immediately visible. Sometimes this approach can lead to unproductive practices such as the establishment of a "culture corner," where artifacts that supposedly represent the cultural background of classroom families are displayed. These items may represent some aspects of the families' cultures (or perhaps ways those cultures once were), but can scarcely capture the complexity of the ways the families interact and live their lives in today's world unless materials are chosen to reflect integral, current aspects of living culture for the social community context in which you teach. Besides identifying meaningful materials that represent and embody the cultural context of the families, you will need to focus on the behavioral dimensions of particular cultures reflected within your classroom.

This second domain of culture is more revealing when you pay attention to the behaviors, or ways of doing things in the homes and in the communities where the families reside. What are the routines for feeding, sleeping, and other self-help tasks of daily life in the communities that you serve? Learning about the traditions families follow, the activities they pursue during the week and on the weekends, and their occupations (among other things) certainly will expand the picture of similarities and differences among the children in the classroom and their families, and may possibly provide entrées into themes that are fruitful as vehicles for integrating learning in the social studies curriculum. Yet these perspectives may also be limited, in that knowledge of traditions, customs, and actions of families in a social context do not necessarily reveal the deeper motivations for these patterns of behavior.

It is in the third domain—that of values, belief systems, and worldviews—that yields the most fruitful interaction between teachers and their students and families. It is through sensitive understanding of belief systems that you as a teacher can identify and explore with families the areas in which resonance or conflict with the social studies curriculum may appear. It is in this domain that conversations with families may lead to an exploration of the meanings behind common practices and the engagement of children in multiple ways of seeing how the world works around them. Use of this third domain, however, depends on teachers' willingness to build a trusting relationship with families, so that authentic information can be exchanged, as well as on teachers' willingness to explore and reveal their own values and beliefs (Ramsey, 2004).

Drawing on these three domains requires that teachers develop or adopt ways to collect specific cultural information from their own families and from the families of the children in their classrooms, so that they are working with aspects of culture that are recognized and known by various participants in the classroom. Generalizations about cultures that are frequently found in texts may be dated, inaccurate, or otherwise biased in ways that can only perpetuate stereotypes and cultural misunderstandings. Thus, some teachers of young children have worked out ways to do "cultural surveys," including conversations that children can have with family members over something concrete, such as a family photo album, as part of their "homework" (De Gaetano et al., 1998). The results of the conversations are collated by the teacher and suggest themes that can serve to organize a series of social studies lessons or activities. Another teacher has developed family interviews done by the children as part of the daily work in the classroom. The material that comes from these interviews then becomes the center of her social studies curriculum, and all other learning (in the areas of literacy, math, science, art, etc.; Rogovin, 2001).

*Classroom Physical Context.* These practices bring us to consideration of the use of culture in the *context* of social studies teaching and learning. What are the specific contexts that carry culture in classrooms for young children? Once again, there are at least three of these. First, there is the physical environment of the classroom, the ways furnishings are arranged, the inclusion of certain "interest areas" and the particular materials used in them, the ways the room is decorated and children's work is displayed, and the continuing construction of representations of the focus of the children's current inquiry (Kendall, 1997). Examples of the last of these would be the transformation of a classroom's housekeeping/family area into an "animal hospital" by a group of four-year-olds investigating the care of pets after the mother of one of the children gave an interview describing her work as a veterinarian, or using the block area to make a "bagel factory" like the one the five-year-olds had recently visited, in which the father of one of the children was working. Choices (by teachers and children together) made in the preparation of the physical environment convey messages to young children about ways that they might work collaboratively or independently, the value of specific materials that reflect the children's ongoing cultural experiences, and the importance of the work of individual children in showing their grasp of the concepts and skills under investigation (Williams et al., 1985). In the teaching of social studies, identification of the elements to be included in the preparation of the environment comes from marriage of the aims of the social studies curriculum with culturally informed conversations and direct experience in the community; thus, the information acquired through cultural surveys and interviews/family contacts is vitally important to the promotion of social studies learning.

*Classroom Interpersonal Context.* A second context is the interpersonal environment of the classroom. The manners used in the ways teachers address children and children address teachers, the demonstration in classrooms of respect for family members, the courtesies encouraged in children in their interaction with one another, the recognition of possible variation in learning styles and provision of opportunities for their exercise, focus on developing an appreciation for multiple perspectives on an issue, and a spirit of curiosity about the lives of others (Gay, 2000) are all examples of ways that the promotion of children's social learning lies at the heart of a multiculturally oriented social studies curriculum. Expanding children's knowledge and appreciation of variation in customs of courtesy is illustrated in the following occurrence observed in a first-grade classroom.

> The children in Rebecca Scott's first-grade classroom in New York City recently welcomed a new child into their group. The six-year-old girl, Wanda, moved with her family from the coast of Alabama, where a hurricane destroyed the small town where she was born and lived for the first years of her life. She and her family were now sharing a home with her aunt, who moved to the city fifteen years before when she secured a job in her field of health care. When Wanda first came to the classroom, she addressed her teacher as "Ms. Scott," an address she had heard the teacher called by adults in the new school. The teacher told her that she invited the children to call her by her first name, "Rebecca." Wanda persisted in calling Rebecca "Ms. Scott," however, and some of the other children found that to be "silly." When Rebecca overheard a hurtful comment to Wanda about this one day, she took the next opportunity in a class meeting to point out that there were different ways of being polite to people older than yourself in different parts of the country;

and that in many towns in the southern United States, adults expected children to address them more formally than with just a first name. She thanked Wanda for her courtesy and told the children that they all had a choice—they could continue to call her "Rebecca," or they could call her "Ms. Scott" just as Wanda did. She also invited the children to talk with their families about which form of address they preferred. Over the next week, some of the children experimented with using the more formal manner of address. After discussing this with her family, Wanda decided to call her teacher "Miss Rebecca," a form of address traditional in her original community.

Rebecca Scott adjusted the mode of address in her classroom in response to a custom introduced by a child new to the school. She acknowledged that child's social knowledge and used the incident as a way to expand the social repertoires of all the children involved. In a later conversation at a classroom parent get together, she related the discussion with the children as one of the many ways she was addressing the expected social studies content in first grade, centered on "the individual in school and family life."

By working with this moment in the life of the children, Ms. Scott used an opportunity to expand the children's social knowledge also as a context to enable further social development in children having difficulty recognizing that there can be more than one perspective on an issue. She validated Wanda's cultural experience as well as that of the other children, and, in doing so, she enabled all involved to make meaning out of differences in behaviors.

*Classroom Culturally Responsive Content.* The third context that carries culture in the classroom is the infusion of culturally responsive content into all learning activities. Like the other two, this context also relates to the making of meaning. So far, and in the material that follows in this text, social studies is discussed in terms of attitudes, concepts, and skills or processes that further thinking and enable understanding of the ways the social world (the parts that are near to us and those that are distant) works. Through social studies, young children come to appreciate their own roles and the roles of others within society, and they learn to anticipate ways of thinking, being, and acting related to particular outcomes— hopefully toward the improvement of relationships among people and between people and the planet, cooperatively to preserve and develop human and environmental resources in life-producing and consciousness-expanding ways. Examples of such general aims are found in state social studies standards and in Head Start outcomes.

In order for young children to grasp these aims, however, they must see how each new attitude, concept, and skill or process taught relates to what they already have learned through their direct experience with the world, their observation of and interaction with the thoughts, language, and actions of others, and their absorption of the value systems at the foundations of their societies. Thus, the particular examples teachers use to illustrate processes, how recognizable these examples are to the children from their past experience, and the degree to which these examples key into children's interests and impulses are critically important in the making of meaning (Bruner, 1978). An example of building new learning in social studies on familiar frames of reference appears in the following observation:

> In a third-grade classroom, children born and raised in Boston and children whose families came to Boston from various islands in the Caribbean were studying how Boston Harbor shaped the commerce of the city. Looking at the first functions of the harbor from 300 years ago raised comment from the Caribbean children about the exciting legends of piracy associated with the harbors they knew from the Islands. Their teacher, Tim Daniels, picked up on the enthusiastic descriptions of the supposed exploits of famous buccaneers and suggested that the class do a comparative study of two or three of the famous Caribbean harbors with Boston Harbor. In what ways were the histories and functions of harbors in the two sites similar? In what way were they different? With Mr. Daniels' skillful leadership, the children explored the role geography played in the evolving functions of the harbors and the connection between goods available at each location and the growing sea trade. This focus brought children to the library and Internet, where, inevitably, the history of enslavement was foregrounded. Now the children were beginning to discover the "Golden Triangle"—the trade of human beings from Africa, for Caribbean sugar, for New England rum, and back again. The horror and injustice of what occurred in the past began to be addressed by the children. A few of the children began to question whether these events were related to ways some people in their city acted toward each other around issues of jobs, police actions, or housing. They wondered who was doing something about these tensions and if there was a way they could help those trying to relieve them. Clearly they entered upon an inquiry that could potentially last all year and would lead to first constructions of what might be meant by "social justice." During the encounter, the children embarked on the beginnings of a complex investigation that could be revisited with increasing sophistication in Grades 4 onward.

The power of this unfolding social studies curriculum for the children was undeniable. What began as a relatively lighthearted look at piracy (the reality of which was far different from the romantic notions the children held and could bear its own inquiry) transformed into a serious exploration of one of the great human tragedies. At the third-grade level, the children of course were not expected to uncover all or even the greater part of the complex interactions involved in these historical events. Still, they were beginning to raise important questions and, in subsequent conversations, to see connections between those events and the racial tensions that surfaced periodically in their city. They also were beginning to develop their own positions and identities around issues of injustice. In what ways could they become future advocates for humankind and resist modern oppressions in their community?

The instances described above represent some of the many ways that multicultural perspectives and approaches can extend and deepen the social studies curriculum. This leads to a closer examination of how these aspects work in interaction with the desired outcomes for the social studies curriculum.

## Multicultural Perspectives and Approaches to Social Studies: Enacting Standards through Cultural Awareness

The terms *multicultural perspectives* and *multicultural approaches* are used synonymously in some texts exploring multicultural educational practice. In other texts, however, there is a distinction, which can prove useful in curriculum planning.

### Multicultural Perspectives

*Multicultural perspectives* can be understood to refer to a vision of *who* is to be served by the effort, combined with differentiated *aims* for those populations. Christine Sleeter and Carl Grant[2] (1987, 1999) have explored such multicultural perspectives over the past three decades by reviewing the burgeoning multicultural educational literature and classifying it into five basic categories: (1) Education for the Exceptional and Culturally Different, (2) Single-Group Studies (formerly called Ethnic Studies), (3) Human Relations, (4) Multicultural Education, and (5) Education That Is Multicultural and Social Reconstructionist. While various ones of these have appeared or been emphasized at different points in time, all five continue to appear in the literature to the present day, and curriculum planners should be aware of the differences among them in drawing upon such resources in their work.

*Education for the Exceptional and Culturally Different.* The first category refers to works that have been designed to address the learning needs of children whose cultural experience is outside of the norms expected in public schooling and whose academic achievement may consequently be depressed. The works usually reference the acquisition of attitudes, concepts, and skills that will enable the children to succeed in school.

*Single-Group Studies.* The second category is directed toward members of particular cultural groups who wish to deepen their understanding of the elements of their own cultures. Such materials may also be used by people wishing to learn the particulars of a culture that is different from their own. The works are focused on description of elements of a specific culture and attempt to reveal the meanings of those elements for members of the cultural group.

*Human Relations.* The third category is intended for people whose cultural group affiliations have placed them in conflict with members of other groups. The materials are intended to develop ways to reduce tensions among groups and create an atmosphere of mutual respect, knowledge, and cooperation.

*Multicultural Education.* The fourth category moves significantly beyond the first three in that it is designed for all children and adults, to foster appreciation for cultural differences, and to encourage an active and positive curiosity about differences, as well as recognition of essential similarities in the life ways of varying cultural groups.

*Multicultural and Social Reconstructionist.* Finally, the fifth category extends the fourth to include acquisition of individual and group advocacy skills in addressing issues of social justice. These latter materials rest on the premise that society itself needs to be critiqued toward elimination of oppressive practices against members of particular cultural groups. In integrating multicultural perspectives into the teaching of social studies, the fourth and fifth categories would seem to be those that most clearly resonate with the purposes of the Social Studies Standards and Head Start Outcomes.

As the Standards and Outcomes of social studies focus largely on processes (see Chapter 3 of this book), they can be addressed through the design of learning contexts (physical environments, interpersonal interactions, and content of activities) that, as previously described, draw on children's cultural and social knowledge. This was seen in the two descriptions of social studies teaching practice included above. Various parts of each of these scenarios can be correlated to particular Social Studies Standards. Thus, the learners make meaning within their cultural contexts, while also expanding their learning to include new concepts, skills, and attitudes in the full social studies arena. Without such an integration of multicultural perspectives into the teaching of social studies, teachers run the danger of limiting the number and kinds of connections that children may make in their exploration of the wider social world.

## Multicultural Approaches

Integrating multicultural perspectives into the teaching of social studies requires an awareness of *multicultural approaches* to social studies curriculum design. James Banks (1999) describes a common sequence of professional engagement by those working toward a full use of multicultural perspectives. He suggests that there are four levels of practice showing increasing command of the intentions and aims of multiculturalism in education. Perusal of these levels of practice reveals their applicability in considering the ways we can strengthen our multicultural orientation in the teaching of social studies.

*The Contributions Approach.* Identified by Banks as Level 1 is the first attempt at integration. In this approach, social studies teachers seek out examples of particular people or events that have not traditionally been a part of social studies learning activities. An example of this might be a kindergarten teacher's inclusion of African American and female inventors in the children's study of inventions in the United States that had previously featured only White (European American) men. Little changes otherwise are made in the presentation of the curriculum.

*The Additive Approach.* The second level of multicultural educational practice is called the *additive approach.* Here teachers still retain the traditional structure of their social studies curriculum, but add themes, concepts, or perspectives that represent specific cultural knowledge from groups not previously represented in the curriculum. For instance, a second-grade teacher might add examples of the many ways that children around the world make and play with kites in a unit on "Children's Play" (part of the focus on "The Neighborhood"). Now the children are being introduced to neighborhoods around the world that use variations of a favorite game. This level is still a process of accretion, rather than a change responsive to all three domains of culture.

*The Transformational Approach.* Banks calls the third level the *transformational approach.* Now teachers take a deeper look at the structure of their social studies curriculum and consider ways that variation in cultural behaviors and worldviews (belief systems, values) might be incorporated into social studies inquiries. Ms. Scott's work with first graders described earlier is an example of at least a beginning level of curriculum transformation. This work could also be considered to be an instance of multicultural practice as described by Sleeter and Grant (1999).

*The Social Action Approach.* The fourth level of multicultural educational practice Banks identifies as the *social action approach.* In this deeper and more complex undertaking, teachers not only transform the structure of their social studies curriculum, but also work with the children to identify arenas where the class can take action to address oppressive social conditions. An example of this approach is the inquiry into Boston Harbor facilitated by Mr. Daniels. In the course of their inquiry, the third-graders encountered the history of enslavement in the United States and its connections to trade with the Caribbean and Africa. This led them to think about what it means to be enslaved, and some of the children made the connection between the past situation and racial tensions that periodically surface in their urban setting. The children began to consider ways that they, who were members of a racially and culturally mixed community, could find out about the work being done to help ease such tensions and discover if there was some way they could join the effort. They were entering one of the broader arenas of social studies.

## The Broader Arena of Teaching Social Studies: Beyond Tolerance to Awareness of the Wider World

Often, when teachers think of the role of multicultural practice in the teaching of social studies, specialized curricula such as the *Anti-Bias Curriculum* (Derman-Sparks and the A.B.C. Task Force, 1989), a focus on multicultural education as social activism (pursuit of *social justice*; Lewis, 1991; Sleeter, 1996), or an emphasis on *global education* (Swiniarski, Breitborde, & Murphy, 1999) come to mind. However, throughout this chapter, there are illustrations that show the infusion of multicultural perspectives into the social studies curriculum, which is actually a broader undertaking. Such approaches have multiple aims that resonate with the aims of social studies and with the various perspectives and approaches already described. Banks (1999), for example, sees five dimensions to the broader involvement of multicultural education:

1. *Content Integration.* This dimension refers to the use of examples from the children's cultures to illustrate concepts and skills being taught. The purpose is the enable all children to connect with the content in ways that further the processes of their meaning-making.

2. *Knowledge Construction.* This dimension challenges single frames of reference in making meaning and invites students to investigate other perspectives.

3. *Equity Pedagogy.* This dimension refers to teachers' changing their pedagogy to include varieties of learning styles and dispositions related to children's ability to absorb and work with content.

4. *Prejudice Reduction.* This dimension focuses on enabling children to change their negatives attitudes toward people, places, or events.

5. *Empowering School Culture and School Structure.* This dimension refers to confronting institutionalized biases and working toward their elimination and, thus, the elimination of oppression, which can inhibit children's achievement.

In Ms. Scott's activity, you can see the use of the aims of knowledge construction, prejudice reduction, and creating an empowering school culture. In Mr. Daniels' work, the aims of content integration, knowledge construction, and again the creation of an empowering school culture were evident. Each of these teachers were also combining these practices with the aims of specific social studies standards in a complementary foundation for their work.

There are times, however, when teachers may choose to focus on the aims of prejudice reduction and empowerment through the use of a very particular curriculum, such as the *Anti-Bias Curriculum* (Derman-Sparks and the A.B.C. Task Force, 1989). Resources such as this suggest ways for teachers of young children to confront prejudices in a concentrated effort. At other times, teachers may want to develop in the children an awareness of issues of *social justice* (teaching children to recognize oppressions affecting themselves or others) and encourage a disposition toward taking social action to address these issues. Teachers then may draw upon specialized resources for such work (Lewis, 1991) within the larger social studies curriculum. The same can be said for a focus on *global education,* when teachers turn children's attention to similarities and differences in the concerns of social studies across the world. The aim here is developing in children a consciousness of being citizens of the world. There is a clear movement within social studies curriculum development today toward creating such an awareness, as many see globalization as an inevitable future for which children today must be prepared.

Use of these resources alone, however, do not constitute having a multiculturally oriented social studies curriculum. Instead, the broader efforts described in this chapter provide the deep and lasting multicultural foundation for social studies that educators seek in many program evaluations today.

## Assessing Achievement in Social Studies: Issue of the Pervasive Influence of Culture

A whole chapter in this text is devoted to the concerns of assessment of children's achievement in the area of social studies. However, to emphasize the importance of cultural knowledge and sensitive application of the principles described above, you should remember that appropriate assessment of young children occurs in a context of deep understanding and application of cultural knowledge in particular classroom situations. In this way, an authentic assessment of children's achievement within a social studies curriculum is undergirded with a multicultural perspective that requires attention to the contexts that children draw upon in their responses. Children will learn to move between various contexts, and this tendency needs to be recognized in assessment techniques and instruments used. Thus, the use of standardized assessments alone is unlikely to be adequate to represent children's acquisition of attitudes and new knowledge and skills through the curriculum. This is particularly true when considering textbook tests and various state and national achievement tests that are drawn from "the typical" rather than the specific aspects of culture that are reflected within your classroom.

## Summary

This chapter reviewed a variety of possibilities for infusing multicultural perspectives throughout the social studies curriculum. What is evident is that using a multicultural orientation to social studies is not a separate effort, but is an effort that should be fully integrated into all aspects of social studies teaching. It is also clear that such use of multicultural understandings is a far broader effort than an isolated or particular focus on an area, such as prejudice reduction, alone. In the chapters that follow, you will see allusion to one or another of the aims for using multicultural perspectives. It is helpful always to keep in mind that these are parts of the larger whole of transformative education.

## Activities in the Field

1. For the community where you live or the one in which you aspire to teach, find out about who lives in the community. Collect information about the traditions, migration patterns, and history of the various subgroups within the community. Identify ways that you would connect with the families as an early childhood teacher.

2. With a colleague, interview an elder in the community. Identify the school experiences that promoted acceptance in the community as well as any experiences that created tension or negative relations in the community.

## Activities in the Library

1. Begin an annotated bibliography of children's books that will promote positive views of diverse cultural groups in your community. Start by examining the annual list of notable books from the National Council for Social Studies.

2. Examine the standards for social studies for your state. Identify ways to connect various meaningful cultural activities to these standards for your community.

## Study Questions

1. How is culture manifest in the lives of young children and their families?

2. How does a child's culture influence acquisition of social studies dispositions, knowledge, and skills?

3. What are the best ways to incorporate multicultural appreciation and particular cultural understandings in the early childhood curriculum?

4. How do you connect cultural knowledge and experiences to state standards and Head Start outcomes?

5. In what ways are antibias curricula, teaching for social justice, and global education connected to the approaches that promote multicultural understandings?

6. What important understandings about particular cultures contribute to sound practices in assessment of young children?

## Reflect and Re-read

1. Why is understanding the concept of culture and knowledge about specific cultures so important to teachers of young children?

2. How can early childhood teachers demonstrate to families that they are serious about respect for diversity in the classroom?

3. In what ways does knowledge of culture and specific social–cultural contexts contribute to the development of the social studies program?

## Notes

1. Recently biologists have posited that some of the higher apes have developed cultures (such as the use of tools to acquire food), which juveniles in each generation learn from adults, and some other animals may have done so as well. We therefore can no longer claim that culture is a uniquely human creation.

2. Sleeter and Grant do use the term *approaches* in some of their works exploring these perspectives.

## Suggested Readings

Gorski, P. C. (2005). *Multicultural education and the Internet: Intersection and integrations. 2nd ed.* Boston, MA: McGraw-Hill. This book has annotated website information and illustrative lesson plans.

Ramsey, P. G., & Williams, L. R. (with E. B. Vold). (2003). *Multicultural education: A source book* (2nd ed.). New York: Routledge Falmer. This is a compilation of resources related to multicultural perspectives on various aspect of early childhood education.

Rogovin, P. (1998). *Classroom interviews: A world of learning.* Portsmouth, NH: Heinemann. This book shows how to use interviews as a method of learning the social studies.

Tiedt, P. L., & Tiedt, I. M. (2006). *Multicultural teaching: A handbook of activities, information, and resources* (7th ed.). Boston, MA: Allyn & Bacon. A resource that links theory with examples of best practice.

## References

Banks, J. A. (1999). *An introduction to multicultural education* (2nd ed.). New York: Teachers College Press.

Bruner, J. (1978). *The relevance of culture.* Cambridge, MA: Harvard University Press.

De Gaetano, Y., Williams, L. R., & Volk, D. (1998). *Kaleidoscope: A multicultural approach for the primary school classroom.* Upper Saddle River, NJ: Merrill/Prentice Hall.

Derman-Sparks, L., and the A.B.C. Task Force. (1989). *Anti-bias curriculum: Tools for empowering young children.* Washington, DC: National Association for the Education of Young Children.

Gay, G. (2000). *Culturally responsive teaching: Theory, research and practice.* New York: Teachers College Press.

Kendall, F. E. (1996). *Diversity in the classroom: New approaches to the education of young children.* New York: Teachers College Press.

Lewis, B. A. (1991). *The kids' guide to social action: How to solve the social problems you choose—And turn creative thinking into positive action* . Minneapolis, MN: Free Spirit.

Mead, M. (1935). *Sex and temperament: In three primitive societies* (p. 322). London: George Routledge & Sons, Limited.

Ramsey, P. G. (2004). *Teaching and learning in a diverse world* (3rd ed.). New York: Teachers College Press.

Rogovin, P. (2001). *The research workshop: Bringing the world into your classroom.* Portsmouth, NH: Heinemann.

Sleeter, C. E. (1996). *Multicultural education as social activism.* Albany, NY: State University of New York Press.

Sleeter, C. E., & Grant, C. A. (1987). An analysis of multicultural education in the United States. *Harvard Educational Review, 57*(4), 421–444.

Sleeter, C. E., & Grant, C. A. (1999). *Making choices for multicultural education: Five approaches to race, class, and gender* (3rd ed.). Columbus, OH: Merrill/Prentice Hall.

Swiniarski, L. A., Breitborde, M., & Murphy, J. (1999). *Educating the global village: Including the young child in the world.* Columbus, OH: Merrill/Prentice-Hall.

Williams, L. R., De Gaetano, Y., Harrington, C. C., & Sutherland, I. R. (1985). *ALERTA: A multicultural, bilingual approach to teaching young children.* Menlo Park, CA: Addison-Wesley.

## Web Sites

Asia Source: http://askasia.org. Compilation of Web sources.

Kids Web-Japan: http://web-japan.org/kidsweb/.

MarcoPolo. Social studies and language arts integrated: http://www.marcopolo-education.org.

Oyate: http://www.oyate.org.

Smithsonian Museum: http://www.si.edu/.

Teaching Tolerance, an Internet resource of the Southern Poverty Law Center: http://www.tolerance.org.

U.S. Citizenship and Immigration Services: http://uscis.gov/graphics/aboutus/history/teacher/index.htm.

## CHAPTER 5

# Perspectives on Positive Classroom Practices

Linda Davey and Doris Pronin Fromberg

Every opportunity that occurs within practical activities for developing curiosity and susceptibility to intellectual problems should be seized. John Dewey (1933)

## Terms to Know

- Concentric circles approach
- Disciplines-based approach
- Dynamic themes-based approach
- Holiday-based approaches
- Postmodern-based approach
- Global education

## Overview

This chapter considers how to connect young children's experiences and readiness for learning new social knowledge with adult understandings of social life and the social sciences from a variety of perspectives. The chapter describes a critical-pedagogy approach to thinking about curriculum and planning. The authors assume that young children are capable of understanding and imagining concepts and issues that range beyond a narrow focus on isolated facts. Therefore, this chapter presents an image of young children who are capable of constructing connections across disciplines that begin with authentic social experiences. This is a child-centered and experiential approach. The chapter explicates this approach with classroom examples.

## Focus Questions

1. What are different approaches to teaching young children social studies?
2. How can teachers match adult understandings of social studies concepts with young children's ways of learning?
3. What is global education for young children?

## Diverse Perspectives on Classroom Practices

Often you see in classrooms an approach to social studies that some teachers use which is a *ritualized holiday-centered curriculum*, following the calendar. This approach typically does not focus on the study of the social significance that holidays represent, nor does it include the myriad of holidays represented by the children and families in particular classroom contexts. This superficial approach to planning is in contrast to one that utilizes young children's experiences and knowledge of the world to consider broader cultural issues across the United States and the world. For example, a multicultural study of the social significance of holidays would pursue global holidays clustered together on the basis of the underlying shared human experiences, such as the striving for independence and freedom (young children understand issues of power and powerlessness); the celebration of harvests, an appreciation of abundant food; or the memorializing of heroes and heroines, an opportunity for children to acquire social knowledge about those who modeled helpful work.

Less often, some early childhood teachers focus on a *disciplines-based approach*, that deals with predetermined basic key concepts of social science disciplines. This discipline-based approach is usually derived from the state learning standards. However, young children can better access the processes of the social studies rather than the stated identified key concepts. For example, the historian deals with the interpretation of events. Young children are capable of considering alternative perceptions, that is, the approaches of historians. Geographers consider spatial relationships and how human beings live in relation to different environments.

Young children become geographers as they see contrasts between ur-ban/suburban/rural densities and various landforms in their immedi-ate communities. Economicists study concepts such as scarcity, including needs and wants versus supply and demand. Young children have direct personal experience with the distinction between needing and wanting. Political scientists consider the uses of power and the nature of democracy. Young children engage in daily issues of fairness, power, and powerless-ness. Thus, the skillful, socially conscious teacher can take the discipline-based perspective and build upon the real-life experiences of children to engage them in conceptually sophisticated learning. One way to imple-ment this contextual approach is through the use of *dynamic themes*, which integrates the social studies and social science across the curriculum with the sciences, arts, literacy, and mathematics (Fromberg, 2002). Dynamic themes such as cyclical change, conflict/contrast, and synergy subsume the various social sciences and social learnings providing rich, sophisti-cated contextual curricular opportunities.

This is in contrast to the typical traditional approach to the teaching of social studies, which involves the introduction of curriculum through spheres of learning. These spheres expand with the development of the child from a study of self and primary social groups in the early years, through state and national issues, and finally to a focus on interna-tional curriculum issues in the latter part of elementary school (Larkins & Hawkins, 1990). This *concentric circles approach* to social studies instruc-tion is widely used by teachers, although it is frequently updated with a focus on the identification of "big ideas" that reflect the particular class-room context and the children's knowledge and experience with the social world.

In contrast with the concentric circles approach is the postmodern con-tention that young children will learn about the here-and-now without school instruction and that they can use their imaginations to consider the far away in time and place (Egan, 1999). This *postmodern viewpoint* focuses on children's powers to consider opposing concepts that they have ex-perienced directly before they reach organized schooling; concepts such as "good and bad, love and hate, power and oppression, joy and fear, and so on [the foundation that prepares children for more sophisticated concepts, such as] struggling for autonomy against oppression, ... greed and generosity, [and] ... courage and cowardice" (p. 138). In effect, these underlying, initially socioemotional, concepts help children make con-nections with similar concepts that are far away in time and place. An emerging alternative to these approaches uses research on affective and cognitive development to emphasize a more interdisciplinary approach to the social studies, including *global perspectives*, at every grade level (Swiniarski & Breitborde, 2003). Consider the following recent classroom experience:

> Will enters his Pre-K classroom with a bag under his arm. He takes his place in the circle and Ms. Gumble nods to him: "Will, would you like to tell everyone about what you have in the bag?" "My mom just brought me this from China," he says, as he pulls out a small children's picture book, written in Chinese. Below the printed story lines on each page is one Chinese character, and next to it a model of how to draw that character, step by step. Several hands go up as children chime in, "I've seen that writing before on TV," "My dad's been to China," and "Did she see a panda?" The teacher takes note of the knowledge base conveyed through the children's questions. After a short, animated discussion, Will pulls out a page of Chinese characters that he has drawn from the book's examples and explains how he did them. The teacher asks the children if they too would like to make some characters and they respond enthusiastically. She has previously copied some of the pages of Will's book—and after having Will demonstrate one, she introduces the new materials she has placed in the Writing Center.
>
> Ms. Gumble was helped by the advanced notice that Will's mother offered in a recent email, asking if she was interested in Will's bringing the book to class. Ms. Gumble asked the mother to scan and email some of the pages. In addition, Ms. Gumble conducted some online research, including translating the characters. A world map and globe are permanent as well as familiar fixtures of her classroom and the children explored where China was in relation to their homes. Ms. Gumble will observe the children today and will then consider how much interest there is in the topic, and whether it may be extended into other curriculum centers.

The above scenario illustrates clearly that young children today, particularly middle-class children and children of recent immigrants, are generally more aware of the wider world beyond their immediate communities than they were at anytime in the past. It also illustrates a changing mode of parent–teacher communication. For the most part, this example highlights the influences of transportation and technology. These in turn have had a major impact on communication and economic relationships, and encourage new global insights on issues of peace, the environment, justice, equity, diversity, and interdependence. To illustrate the child relevant perspective on planning, several samples studies are presented: first, a study of transportation; then a study of community; and, finally, a study of how environmental changes, beginning with the observations of pond life, influence human life.

## A Study of Transportation

The way that travel influences children's perception of the world is worth considering for those who have the opportunity to travel. Concepts of space, time, and speed are all adjusted when children board a plane at one point and get off at another, for example. Although the world of children who have had access to airplane travel may have shared some experiences, geographical changes in cultural habits are still readily visible to children who travel or view some television programs (smaller cars in Europe or people living in caves and boats in China, for example.) Adults think little of such mental adjustments, having already dealt with these changes, but for children, a shifting in their worldviews, even if unvoiced, is taking place. Another example is that the concept of "mapping" takes on more cognitive significance when a child can view a city grid, a highway, farmland, or a coastline from a mountain top, the roof of a tall building, or most clearly, from the air. Certainly, mapping has more congruence with children's lives and perceptions when the ground surfaces are viewed from a distance. At the same time, children in low-income families in the United States are less likely to have had the advantages of airplane travel and acquaintance with distant countries except, perhaps, by viewing television programs. Nevertheless, teachers can add to the images of distant places and times for children through the use of picture files.

The development of picture files (see box p. 84) as a teaching tool or for the children as a resource is a wise use of time and energy that can help prompt discussion of children's experiences and further their opportunities to acquire new meanings of distant places and times.

Effective teachers help children make connections by providing motivation for children to build new meanings. Examine the opportunities for meaning-making in the example below:

## Transportation around the World: Grade—Prekindergarten or Kindergarten

### Week's Focus: More Alike Than Different

**Monday:** After a neighborhood walk or focused observations from classroom windows, children can discuss how people travel. Then, they can select pictures showing local transportation as well as modes of travel throughout the world (elephant, canoe). Look also for photographs of local travel children might not readily identify (horse and buggy in Central Park or performer on an elephant in the circus) and common modes of transportation elsewhere (jets in

### Picture Files

A helpful asset for any teacher is a good picture file. It can be created over time, and is most useful if it is kept in a place where both teacher and children can access it freely and easily. It can be a great resource for teachers when planning lessons or themes and for children when they are block building, writing, drawing, and discussing. For a file to be really useable, it must be well organized right from the start. If the box is organized by topic, then new additions can easily be dropped into the appropriate category with little time wasted. Housing the picture file in the Block/Construction Area invites use by pre-kindergarten through primary-grade children, and often stimulates block (and other) play corresponding to the subject of study:

- Begin with a "box" to hold pictures, up to an 8 × 10-inch size. (Larger selections may create a space problem.) Label it boldly.

- Create dividers corresponding to major themes such as Families, Communities, Shelter, Food, Clothing, Transportation, Communication, etc. (Dividers should be larger than 8 × 10 inches so that category titles are visible.)

- Look for pictures in magazines, newspapers, art and history books, as well as teachers' guides that might be useful for children to explore. (In *Transportation*, for example, look for photographs or artwork depicting methods of transportation, both past and present: people walking, riding on donkeys or in sampans, Viking boats, steam ships, horse and buggies, cars, rocket ships, etc.)

- Enlarge and copy selections, if necessary, so that they more easily capture children's attention and are relatively uniform in size. Provide backing to pictures for ease of handling.

- Supplement your selections with photos you take yourself. This allows flexibility not only to fill in gaps in your collection, but personalizes the experience (e.g. a photo of your great-grandfather in his first car.). Local examples and historical society archives can also prove interesting to children. (A photo of an existing street in your school's community with horse and buggies, contrasted with a current photo of the same street, can provoke some interesting and thoughtful discussions.)

- Provide illustrations that offer multiple viewpoints (e.g., from the top of a building and the bottom, from a plane window and looking up at a plane flying).

- Include any informational details on the back of the picture: year, location, citation, artist, etc., for help in answering children's questions.

- Add to your collection as you come across interesting pictures, but especially when you are planning thematic content.

- Highlight and display (on a small easel or in a learning center) topical illustrations that pertain to current classroom themes.

China). Have globe/map to refer to as you discuss countries and regions.

**Tuesday:** Using pictures previously displayed on the bulletin board, ask children how transportation around the world is similar and different (raise hands and tally perspectives). Discuss examples.

**Wednesday:** Ask children how they travel with their families (car, bus, subway, plane). It takes money to travel those ways. Why? How would they travel if they didn't have money? If their religion didn't allow it (Amish picture)? How would climate influence the ways they would travel (pictures of yaks or dogsleds)? Discuss.

**Thursday:** Read *From Camel Cart to Canoe* (Noonan, 1992). Use the globe and consider transportation in other countries. What is alike? What is different? Why?

**Friday:** Give children a selection of photos of transportation throughout the world. Each will choose two to glue onto paper and dictate whether people travel that way because of climate, geography, money, tourism, or custom. Discuss: Are we more alike or different? (Adapted from Alleman & Brophy, 2002, pp. 191–195)

## Looking at Teacher Planning for Social Studies

Teachers plan thoughtfully to consider ways in which children can engage in direct experiences. Hands-on activities connect to children's realities, including some familiar materials and ideas, while extending those ideas with new experiences. Teachers help children fit new information into their existing mental structures or cognitive maps. Teachers help children expand their understandings of the world into ever-widening spheres that reach young children's store of knowledge about the world through television, photographs, and books. However, facts, vocabulary, and even language have little use without connection to previously acquired knowledge and experiences. Therefore, teachers try to help children make connections that allow each child to integrate and access understandings of the world and how each fits into the community where they live and the world at large. The teacher tries to assess the children's prior knowledge and tries to integrate learning activities along with meaning.

The transportation example above offers ideas from one week's lessons of a much longer, sequentially based study that incorporates preassessment and revisiting, as well as many attempts to connect to children's understanding of concepts. It is focused in its goals and therefore can authentically promote and assess children's learning. The "Big Picture" question that drives the investigation,"How is it similar and how is it different?" is the type of question that has many applications in various other contexts and which draws children into problem solving as a reason for learning.

Looking at the example of a study of transportation addresses the social impact of resources that are both local and distant. The social studies, in focusing on the social impact of environment and resources, can bring children into an understanding of multicultural issues through such examinations. Some television programs also expose children to diverse characters, such as those in *Sesame Street* and *Dora the Explorer* (which also attempts to infuse the Spanish language seamlessly into the programming) while others present characters and scenes that reflect diversity. Children's understandings of the world are best enhanced, however, when teachers provide children with opportunities to investigate (Katz & Chard, 2000), play (Fromberg, 2002), and converse (Bodrova & Leong, 1996) about activities that capture their interest (Dewey, 1938). Consider the section below that recounts the social studies experience in a kindergarten classroom.

## An Emergent, Meaningful Study of the Concept of a Community

### The Kindergarten Setting

The block area is not a "corner" in this classroom, but a wide space, well provisioned with blocks. When several children became excited about a construction project on their street, children began to represent their observations with floor blocks. Ms. Kuhn allowed the construction to stand for a few days, so that it could be "revisited" and added to. This also allowed her to bring in books and other activities that added to the children's interest and knowledge as it evolved.

### The Stimulus

Several children were enthralled by construction going on down the block. Ms Kuhn encouraged their block-building with pointed questions, and before long, there were several buildings going up. At the end of the day, she gathered the class around the block area and asked the children what they would have to plan for if those were real buildings in their community of blocks. This led to her remembering that one father was an architect and she asked him in to speak to the children, who showed a great deal of interest in the blueprints he brought with him. In turn, this led to their incorporation of "blueprints" into their block work, then a "drafting table," and, eventually, to a whole class study on "community."

### The Extension

Ms. Kuhn noted that the children's vocabulary became punctuated, not only with the new architectural terms, but with those that identified the blocks themselves: column, pillar, floor board, ramp, Gothic Arch, and Roman Arch. She listened as children built an airport, and discussed the countries where the planes would go. "I want to go to Disneyland," said one child, while another commented, "I want to go see my grandpa in Peru." She flipped through her "Picture File" (discussed earlier) and pulled out photographs of buildings and communities around the world, arranging them to attract children's attention, especially any that matched the children's comments.

As interest progressed, Ms. Kuhn drew the children's attention to the map and globe in the classroom and they explored destinations before comparing distances between those destinations on the map or globe. All over the classroom, activities and projects blossomed, all offshoots of the children's interest.

Materials displayed provoked discussions of how communities differ, how they are the same, and finally returned to the construction down the block and what might be built in the middle of this particular community. "Could it be an airport?" the teacher queried. "Could they build an airport on that construction site?" "What would it need to be an airport?" "Where would people park?" As thoughts tumbled out and children displayed their understandings in words and drawings, block building had another surge of interest and the area became crowded with "community builders."

### Forms of Representations

To relieve congestion, and to extend the experience, Ms. Kuhn moved slowly onto wood constructions with glue and a "planned" community. After lengthy discussions of what every community needed, each child selected a community structure to build, and chose a wood base as a platform for their structures. Work progressed intermittently over several weeks from the gluing table to the painting table to the 7 × 4-foot piece of plywood that would serve as the community. Children sketched and wrote in journals about their building and as each structure took shape, the teacher helped individual children "revisit" their original concept and explore the structure taking shape in light of a growing understanding of that building's form and function, and its place in the community (e.g., "Do you want to place your Fire Department right next to a hospital?")

### Finding/Using Resources, Collaborating

Over lunch in the teacher's room, Ms. Kuhn shared some stories of the children's excitement with the fifth-grade teacher, who asked if her class could "buddy" with the kindergarteners and help them. The fifth-graders came in on a regular basis and helped their kindergarten partners make trees and traffic lights, as well as road and building signs. This one-to-one ratio between partners allowed the teacher to circulate, question, provoke thinking, and offer suggestions in a way that was very productive to her planning and instruction. It allowed space and time for her to problem-solve with children as needed, and was valuable to her ability to authentically assess individual children's learning and their ways of representing their knowledge. On checking further with the parents, the teacher found a female pilot, a postal worker, a librarian, a construction worker, and a politician to come in, talk to the class, and act as consultants about the community being built by the kindergarteners.

### Webbing

Ms. Kuhn's initial plans for this study were very simple. The plans branched out and became more complex as the study evolved. The teacher added concepts as the children's understanding, interest, and involvement grew.

In effect, Ms Kuhn begins with a preliminary plan and modifies it through interactions with the children, assesses their current knowledge, and then plans reasonable next steps. Thus, the planning process is predictably unpredictable yet supremely flexible and adaptive. At the same time, she continuously plans events that are likely to help children extend and deepen their knowledge. Ms Kuhn creates the kind of challenge that blends manageable risk with a reasonable chance for success.

The challenging collaboration within the kindergarten and between the kindergarten and fifth-grade children was an opportunity that emerged

when a sensitive teacher recognized and seized an opportunity to expand meaningful learning that grew from a direct experience. Children
had a variety of ways to represent their understandings that included
block building, wood constructions held together with glue, "blueprint
construction," journal drawing, and journal writing. Before interviewing
the architect, they had the opportunity to plan together the questions to
ask him, which the teacher recorded on a large chart.

At other times, kindergarten children solve the problems of how to operate a restaurant in the Dramatic Play area, create an obstacle course on
the playground, or discuss the benefits of varied pizza toppings for snack,
or make explicit rules for the classroom. These experiences provide opportunities for children to learn to de-center, to bump into the feelings
of others and learn empathy and interdependence. For example, children
collaborate on their representations of experience through sociodramatic
play, role play, and construction projects. They negotiate their differences
with one another, and begin to recognize that others have experiences,
wants, needs, and beliefs that may be different from their own perceptions
and experiences. They also build new strategies for getting along with one
another.

## A Study of How Environmental Change Influences Peoples' Lives

Consider how the set of activities above and then, below, for prekindergarten, kindergarten, and first-grade children encourages them to think,
build meanings, and make real connections to some of the concepts recommended by the National Council for Social Studies (NCSS), which include
interdependence, global understanding, and human needs and wants.

A. **Setting**: Kindergarten, near a pond
   **Activity:** Year-long study of pond life and pollution. Children walk
   to a pond next to the school once a week. The integrated study encompasses science, language arts, math, and social studies. For social studies, the emphasis is on understanding the concepts of *environment*, *pollution*, and *recycling*. Each week the children observe
   the pond, sketch what they see, make predictions, discuss changes
   and "journal" (through dictation) on their observations and questions. Over the school year, they keep track of what materials are
   discarded in the pond and on the shore, and discuss how they got
   there, what happens to the material, whom it can harm (fish, ducks,
   people), and how such items can be recycled. The teacher and the

children have picked up refuse each week from their little area of the pond, and regularly compare their section to areas of the pond that have not been cleaned. The children have charted many of the activities in the classsroom, and a weekly newsletter informs parents of vocabulary that has been introduced, with encouragement to use the new words at home.

B. **Setting:** First Grade

   **Activity:** The teacher collected children's books that represent children from many cultures. . The planned art activities include working with natural dyes, mask making, weaving, and other activities representative of different cultures. The dramatic play area is equipped with a child-sized tortilla press, chopsticks, and clothing representative of other cultures. The classroom materials include an abacus and straw baskets, and she has several "collection boxes" for children to sort consisting of rocks, seed pods, and other natural materials. The room is decorated all year with posters and artifacts depicting other cultures and while she encourages parents to share their cultures with the children, the information they share is not merely "visited" once, but "revisited" and reinforced throughout the year

C. **Setting:** Prekindergarten class

   **Activity:** Class Meeting

   The class meeting is held near the close of every day. Children are encouraged to bring up any problems they are having, such as someone being "mean" to them, any "milestones" such as keeping their temper and talking disagreements through. The teacher acts as intermediary, helping children identify the issues and encouraging other children to help problem-solve, while respecting all children involved and not being subjectively judgmental. During the day, when conflicts arise, the teacher (and sometimes the children) advise the child or children involved, "Why don't you bring that up in Class Meeting?"

Example A (kindergarten near a pond) describes a study aimed at increasing understanding that grows as a result of concrete experiences and the process of "revisiting" for deeper meaning-making. While vocabulary is included, it is introduced as a by-product of the children's actual experience.

Example B (first grade using children's literature) explores children's understandings of others. Knowledge emerges from the materials and activities over time, exposure, and connections as they arise in context. Such an approach produces meaning that can affect attitudes and dispositions authentically.

In example C (class meeting), the teacher creates an environment where children can share differing perspectives, where they can share their feelings in the light of discussion and children have an opportunity to decenter, to learn that other people may have other ways of perceiving and feeling. In this approach, the focus is on learning the reasons for the rules and how individual wants and needs can impact on the wants and needs of others. In a way, learning about wants and needs in an interpersonal sense may be a basis for a later understanding of economic wants and needs.

Culturally sensitive teachers reflect on the following:

- Do the activities, holidays, and celebrations included in the classroom reflect a multitude of cultures, religions, and ethnicities? Does the teacher demonstrate a respect for all traditions? Can these celebrations be related to wider themes that have relevance to children's lives, including issues of fairness, friendship, and family responsibilities?

- Are preconceptions of gender challenged in everyday classroom life: Are both boys and girls asked to carry heavy objects as well as asked to pass out snack? Do children line up without reference to gender? Do the materials in centers invite the participation of any gender (dolls and trucks in both the dramatics area and the block area)? Do books/posters/ textbooks/materials provide egalitarian models?

- Are images of many ethnicities represented in the classroom? Are stereotypic ideas challenged?

- Is power conveyed in ways that preclude questioning and problem solving or do children see the teacher respecting everyone's views?

- Are issues of culture, religion, and ethnicity (an individual's sense of identification that provides a sense of belonging to a reference group; Slonim, 1993) treated both as ways in which different people are alike as well as acknowledging and respecting differences?

Example C (class meeting) begins to deal with some of the interpersonal issues and sources of possible interpersonal conflict or stress in children's lives. As human beings interact with one another and their environments influence their lives, stress is inevitable.

## Dealing with the Effect of Environmental Stress

Caregivers and teachers cannot eradicate the sources of stress from children's lives, but they can provide an environment that helps to prepare children with the tools necessary to cope with many of those stressors. Providing space and time for dramatic play is one way to help children try to cope with environmental upheavals. Some examples follow.

- After the Loma Prieta Earthquake in Northern California, reports of "Earthquake" dramatic play became common. Some teachers responded by telling children there was nothing to fear, while others discreetly (or more directly) changed the focus of the play. Some, however, sensing that the children's play was aimed at getting some control over a frightening situation, joined in the children's play and infused some helpful safety and coping mechanisms ("Quick, come with me to the doorway. It's safer there.") Young children showed that they have achieved some sense of control when they later spontaneously play out preparing for an earthquake, shaking back and forth, and calling, "Earthquake's over." Indeed, observing children's dramatic play is a relevant source of assessing their concerns and thoughts.

- The tragic violence in Columbine High School left confused feelings about schools and guns in the minds of many young children. The endless TV coverage could easily be converted in the minds of some to *many* Columbine incidents. How parents dealt with the news in their own homes also influenced children's views and fears. In that situation, teachers had to weave a fine line between discussing the events to help the children work out their security issues and, at the same time, to respect the wishes of parents who had shielded the news story from their children. After September 11, 2001, children all over the country attempted to understand what had happened. Once again, children picked up on the reactions of the people around them. Of course, the trauma and stress were greater for the children who had experienced it first-hand, or lost someone in the disaster, but the horrifying effects of that event probably escaped no one. One little boy, having watched the first plane burst into flames as it hit the Trade Center while he was having his breakfast a few blocks away from the site, kept trying to comprehend the disequilibrium he felt seeing a plane fly *into* a building, rather than *over* it. He repeatedly questioned his mother about what planes were supposed to do, until he felt satisfied by the sameness of her every response.

- The terrible plight of New Orleans residents, left stranded on their roofs without food, water, or rescue after the Katrina hurricane, may leave questions in the minds of many young children. If adults dwell too much on the threats of the hurricane, it can add to children's stress. However, by talking about ways to control the environment through role playing the building of levees and dams, there is an opportunity to help children feel more control in their lives.

Teachers need to be ready to respond to the unknown and the unexpected, certainly, but they also need to step aside as soon as possible and look for the big ideas connected to such events, so that they can most effectively help children make sense of their world and its peoples, and imagine ways to build confidence in their own capacities in a safe classroom environment.

Kostelnik and colleagues (2001) offer several suggestions for countering stress in the classroom. These include the following:
General Teaching Skills

- Recognize and respect individual coping styles
- Use nonverbal attending skills
- Use effective responding skills
- Maintain ongoing surveillance of all children with regard to threats

A Safe Growth-Enhancing Environment

- Intervene immediately in aggressive encounters.
- Seek out opportunities to make every child feel competent and worthwhile.
- Make every child the object of daily individual focused attention
- Give children opportunities to work out feelings through play.
- Eliminate unnecessary competition ("Musical Chairs" really is still fun for young children when you don't remove chairs!)
- Build in relaxation breaks (fun, exercise, breathing)
- Allow children to participate in conflict resolution
- Promote *divergent thought* (opportunities for alternate solutions)

Preventive Stress-Coping Behaviors in Children

- Coach children on what to do in potentially frightening situations
- Expand children's vocabulary to facilitate communication of feelings
- Help children identify their body sensations when they feel angry, sad, joyful, etc. ("I can tell you are angry because of your frown.")
- Allow children to experience consequences of their actions (when safe to do so) and use those consequences as a discussion starting point instead of punishment.
- Provide some time every day for vigorous exercise.

Support for Loss

- Use appropriate vocabulary when discussing death and dying
- Give accurate information
- Answer children's questions matter-of-factly
- Respect the family's religious explanations
- Provide accurate information about a health-impaired classmate
- Acknowledge the pain of parents' separation and/or divorce

Avoid

- Stereotyping families
- Pushing children to talk when they are not ready
- Looking for a "quick fix"
- Failing to recognize your own limitations
- Being inflexible or insensitive to the needs of parents (financial problems; single parents; teenage parents; stepparents; parents of handicapped, bilingual, or migrant families)

In these various ways, teachers have helped children avoid or cope with stressful situations that are interpersonal as well as environmental, and acquire some of the concepts recommended by the NCSS Standards.

## Planning for the Big Picture

In planning for instruction, teachers must keep in mind various approaches to curriculum noted throughout this text. The planning challenge, then, is to connect learning and create opportunities to help children make meaning from those connections. Lessons, extended studies, and/or themes are explored as part of a "big picture" that children will be exposed to. Some authors have explored themes that include food, clothing, and shelter (Alleman & Brophy, 2001); communication, transportation, and family living (Alleman & Brophy, 2002); and childhood, money, and government (Alleman & Brophy, 2003). These authors point out that a teacher must first consider what the children already understand and focus on what children want to know so that they can plan meaningfully for a particular group of children in a particular context. Educators recommend that teachers employ this approach; it is useful begin with interviews and construct learning opportunities around, and connected to, what children already know (Alleman & Brophy, 2003; Rogovin, 2001). How, then, can teachers help children see a subject such as transportation as a "cultural universal" (Alleman & Brophy, 2002)? Even young children, for example, can grasp concepts related to the importance of transportation, how it has changed over time, how transportation affects a community, as well as what transportation they need in their community, the problems that transportation can insinuate into peoples' lives. Children can do so when they have direct experiences, such as those outlined in the preceding discussions of transportation and community, and environment. While helping children grasp an understanding of such interdependence, teachers of young children also introduce concepts of *global education*.

## What Is Global Education in the Early Childhood Setting?

At its most basic level, global education seeks to provide children with the knowledge, skills, and behaviors that will be a productive influence on their lives in an increasingly complex, interdependent world. It aims to introduce students to the people, cultures, perspectives, accomplishments, and needs of the peoples of the world, as part of the social studies curriculum from the very beginning of school.

Thoughtful educators propose principles to guide the development of a comprehensive global education program. They view global education as a combination of the following:

1. Basic education
2. Lifelong learning
3. Cooperative learning
4. Inclusive of all
5. Education for social action

6. Economic education
7. Involving technology
8. Requiring critical and creative thinking
9. Multicultural education
10. Moral education
11. Supporting a sustainable environment
12. Enhancing the spirit of teaching and learning. (Swiniarski & Breitborde, 2003)

This vision of global education assumes the need for a teacher who is knowledgeable about world issues, is flexible in thinking, open to new ideas, and capable of making connections by using multiple perspectives.

The NCSS standards recognize the importance of introducing some basic understandings in the early years. Accordingly, the standards prescribed experiences in the early grades that allow children opportunities to

1. explore ways that language, art, music, belief systems, and other cultural elements may facilitate global understandings or lead to misunderstanding;
2. give examples of conflict, cooperation, and interdependence among individuals, groups, and nations;
3. examine the effects of changing technologies on the global community;
4. explore causes, consequences, and possible solutions to persistent, contemporary, and emerging global issues, such as pollution and endangered species;
5. examine the relationships and tensions between personal wants and needs and various global concerns, such as the use of imported oil, land use, and environmental protection; and
6. investigate concerns, issues, standards, and conflicts related to universal human rights, such as the treatment of children, religious groups, and the effect of war. (NCSS, 1994)

While young children cannot be expected to fully understand these issues, a curriculum that exposes them to such topics through concrete and authentic experiences discussed in this chapter and earlier chapters can be a building block that will allow deeper understandings in the later grades.

## Summary

This chapter presented a few frameworks for considering social studies education that include the ritual holiday-centered approach, a disciplines-based approach, a dynamic themes approach, a concentric circles approach, a postmodern approach, and a global education approach. Practical examples of young children's experiences that represent themes recommended by the NCSS include transportation, community, and environmental study. There also was discussion of the related concerns of teachers for dealing with children's possible stress through a variety of strategies that included provisions for related dramatic play.

The many approaches to teaching young children social studies support the importance of teachers working to build on young children's capacities for activities that are based upon children's prior experiences by planning to match children's integrated personal, social, and physical experiences with adult understandings of broader social issues and concepts.

## Activities in the Field

1. Watch three children's cartoon shows. Look for signs of nationality and culture. Could these shows make sense to children in other cultures? What do you think will be the global impact of such shared programs?

2. Observe Pre-K–K children working on a computer in the classroom. Is there social interaction? How do the children deal together with technological problems?

3. Interview children about a recent major international news item such as the tsunami of 2004. What details do they know about it? Did their information come from parents, TV, or school? Compare the amount and types of information these children can share to your own childhood experiences.

4. Visit a preschool and a kindergarten classroom. Take note of anything in the environment that supports global explorations and understandings, such as literature, illustrations, and materials.

## Activities in the Library

1. Review several recent issues of one early childhood journal. Look for articles that have a global connection. How does this reflect on the

teacher's understandings of global interconnectedness in the twenty-first century?

2. Visit one of the Web sites suggested in this chapter. What did you learn that could inform your teaching? How did it widen your own knowledge base? What activities would you use with young children to enhance your social studies curriculum?

3. Visit the children's literature section of the library. How easy is it to locate children's books with a global theme? Choose five books and compare them in terms of egalitarian and global education.

4. Invite the librarian to talk about literature related to Rosa Parks. What might be next steps in planning related studies?

## Study Questions

1. How can a teacher help a child deal with stressful situations?

2. How do the traumas of violence and war connect to the social studies curriculum?

3. In what ways does the teacher provide a model for understanding diversity?

4. What are some things a teacher can do to check for and eliminate bias in the classroom?

5. Why is it important for a teacher to value (and plan for) all social interaction as a part of the social studies curriculum?

6. How can a particular classroom provide additional space and time for children to engage in dramatic play?

## Reflect and Re-read

1. Think about some of the major issues facing the world today. What knowledge, skills, and dispositions might you include in the early childhood curriculum in order to lay a foundation for understanding and dealing with such issues?

2. What are some ways to integrate social studies curriculum with the sciences, the arts, reading, writing, and mathematics?

## Suggested Readings

Benson, P. (1986). *Teaching foreign cultures in social studies: Strategies for teaching social studies with a global perspective.* Washington, DC: National Endowment for the Humanities. Suggestions for teaching with a global perspective.

Collins, T. H., & Czarra, F. (1991). *Global primer: Skills for a changing world.* Denver, CO: Center for Teaching International Relations. This book provides activities that relate to global education themes for grades K–9.

DeCou-Landberg, M. (1994). *The global classroom: A thematic multicultural model for the K-6 & ESL classroom: Vols. 1 and 2.* Reading, MA: Addison Wesley Longman.

Milford, S. (1992). *Hands around the world: Three hundred sixty-five creative ways to build cultural awareness and global respect.* Charlotte, VT: Williamson. Presents activities for children in Grades 1–8.

National Council for Social Studies. *Social Studies and The Young Learner* is published six times a year. It is included with membership in NCSS.

Peace Child International. (1994). *Rescue Mission planet earth: A children's edition for Agenda 21.* New York: Kingfisher Books, Grisewood & Dempsey. This book, written by children from around the world, addresses environmental issues as well as accompanying children's activities.

Philips, S. U. (1983). *The invisible culture: Communication in classroom and community on the Warm Springs Indian Reservation.* Prospect Heights, IL: Waveland.

Swiniarski, L. A., & Breitborde, M. L. (2003). *Educating the global village: Including the child in the world.* Upper Saddle River, NJ: Pearson Education Inc. This book provides a knowledge base of global educational issues to early childhood professionals, offers teaching/learning strategies that consider young children's development and learning styles and provides suggestions for home–school–community partnerships.

### Children's Literature

Noonan, D. (1992) *From camel cart to canoe.* New York: Wright Group/ Division of McGraw-Hill.

# References

Alleman, J., & Brophy, J. (2001). *Social studies excursions K–3, Book one: Powerful units on food, clothing, and shelter.* Portsmouth, NH: Heinemann.

Alleman, J., & Brophy, J. (2002). *Social studies excursions K–3, Book two: Powerful units on communication, transportation and family living.* Portsmouth, NH: Heinemann.

Alleman, J., & Brophy, J. (2003). *Social studies excursions K–3, Book three: Powerful units on childhood, money, and government.* Portsmouth, NH: Heinemann.

Bodrova, E., & Leong, D. J. (1996). *Tools of the mind.* Englewood Cliffs, NJ: Prentice-Hall.

Dewey, J. (1933). *How we think.* Boston: D.C. Heath

Dewey, J. (1938/1979). *Experience and education.* New York: Collier-Macmillan.

Egan, K. (1999). *Children's minds, talking rabbits, and clockwork oranges.* New York: Teachers College Press.

Fromberg, D. P. (2002). *Play and meaning in early childhood education.* Boston, MA: Allyn & Bacon.

Katz, L. G., & Chard, S. C. (2000). *Engaging children's minds: The Project approach* (2nd ed.). Stamford, CT: Ablex.

Kostelnik, M. J., Whiren, A., Soderman, A. & Stein, L. (2001). *Guiding children's social development.* 4th ed. Clifton Park, NY: Thomson/Delmar.

Kuhn, J. (2005, March). *Integrated community study.* Presentation at the Hofstra New Teachers Network Conference, Hempstead, NY.

Larkins, A. G., & Hawkins, M. L. (1990). Trivial and noninformative content in primary grade social studies texts: A second look. *Journal of Social Studies Research, 14,* 25–32.

National Council for Social Studies. (1994). *Curriculum standards for social studies: Expectations for excellence.* Washington, DC: National Council for Social Studies.

Rogovin, P. (2001). *The research workshop: Bringing the world into your classroom.* Portsmouth, NH: Heinemann.

Slonim, M. B. (1993). *Children, culture, and ethnicity.* New York: Garland.

Swiniarski, L. A., & Breitborde, M. (2003). *Educating the global village: Including the child in the world.* Upper Saddle River, NJ: Merrill/Prentice Hall.

## Web Sites

Education Standards: http://edstandards.org/Standards.html. Includes most state standards.

Explore the Globe Program: http://www.globe.gov/fsl/welcome.html.

Fact Monster: http://www.factmonster.com/. This is an encyclopedia for children.

Global Classroom: http://www.global-classroom.com/.

NCSS Standards and Position Papers: http://www.ncss.org/standards/home.html.

NCSS Criteria for Scope and Sequence: http://www.ncss.org/standards/positions/scope.html.

NCSS Teacher Resources and Lesson Plans: http://www.ncss.org/resources/home.html.

Tales of Wonder: http://www.darsie.net/talesofwonder/. Children's stories by regions and countries.

The Say Hello to the World Project: http://www.ipl.org/youth/hello/. Lists languages and includes an audio clip of the word "hello" in different languages.

Universal Declaration of Human Rights (1948). United Nations Web site: http://www.un.org/Overview/rights.html.

## CHAPTER 6

# Multimedia, the World, and Young Children

I do not fear computers. I fear the lack of them. Isaac Asimov

## Terms to Know

- Big ideas
- Concept loading
- Digital divide
- Information access
- Mapmaking
- Prop boxes
- Readability
- Media literacy

## Overview

Setting up the classroom environment, equipping the room, and choosing the materials to implement the topics of study require consideration of many factors simultaneously. First, consider the learners and their previous learning experiences. Next, focus on the national and state standards to address in the social studies curriculum. Organize the learning in integrated units around "big ideas," those ideas that foster the development of enduring conceptual knowledge. Then, choose the materials and organizational structure to support instruction. Consider the relevant media.

## Focus Questions

1. How do you set the stage to support social studies learning?
2. Which toys, texts, literature, symbols, and classroom equipment do you choose?
3. What role do social studies texts play in the curriculum?
4. How can children's literature, both fiction and nonfiction, support the acquisition of social studies knowledge, skills, and aptitudes?
5. How do you add specialized materials of social studies—maps, globes, reference books—to the curriculum? What do you do with these materials?
6. What role do graphs, diagrams, and other graphic organizers play in social studies?
7. How do you use video, computers, and mass media in the social studies curriculum?
8. What are the issues of power and equity when using multimedia?

## Setting the Stage for Learning: Building an Environment to Integrate Social Studies into the Curriculum

The content of social studies is holistic, that is, focused on the development of conceptual understandings around the ten themes of

1. *Culture as a theme* includes ways that human needs transcend societies.
   - Activities and materials that advance this theme comprise language, stories, folktales, music, and artistic creations of diverse cultures. Family life offers a natural focus for this theme in the early years.
2. *Time, continuity, and change* as a theme examines history and policy actions of a society.
   - Activities and materials include the past, present, and future using letters, diaries, maps, textbooks, and photos. Community and state history and current events are features of this theme.
3. *People, places, and environments* as a theme focuses on the interaction of people and the earth.

- Activities and materials include interpretation of maps, globes, photographs, and charts and expository reading. Land use, weather, recycling, and current events related to natural disasters anchor this theme in the early years.

4. *Individual development and identity* as a theme explores physical development and personal interests.

   - Activities and materials that support this theme include stories about children and families, event analysis, and cooperative learning. Typical themes for exploration are self, family, classroom community, and school life.

5. *Individuals, groups, and institutions* as a theme explores the way in which group members interact in home, school, and community. Rudimentary understanding of government begins in the early years with this theme.

   - Activities and materials include classroom rule development, conflict resolution, stories that highlight the role of community helpers, elections, and political issues. Typical foci include getting along in the classroom, school, and neighborhood; study of community and relevant current events such as elections, bond issues for new schools, and community services.

6. *Power, authority, and governance* as a theme focuses on the issues of governmental structure, the rights of individuals, and concepts such as justice, equity, and fairness.

   - Materials and activities that support this theme include community safety; descriptions of local, state, and national government; cooperative learning; and dispute resolution. Topics typically explored include the local community, the state, and methods for communication.

7. *Production, distribution, and consumption* as a theme explores the ways that societies organize to supply their needs for goods and services.

   - Activities and materials that support this theme include a focus on needs and wants; supply and demand; banks and money; businesses in the community and region. Typical themes for study include money, production of goods and services, and current events related to economic issues, for example, the rise in bus fare.

8. *Science, technology, and society* as a theme focuses on the contribution of science and technology to family life, transportation, communication, and the social significance of endangered species.

- Activities and materials include examination of the tools of a society for homemaking, child care, work, transportation, and communication. Typical themes to explore include childhood across time or around the world as well as the ways to move people and the ways in which people communicate.

9. *Global connections* as a theme includes ways that societies negotiate difference, the effect of technology on the global community, tensions across societies regarding needs and wants, and universal human rights.

   - Activities and materials supporting this theme include exploration of the language, art, music and belief systems of diverse societies here and abroad, and examination of current issues such as oil, land use, protected species, and the treatment of children around the world. Typical theme investigation by young children will depend on the situational context but certainly includes investigations of particular societies nationally and internationally.

10. *Civic ideals and practice* as a theme focuses on the development of citizens.

    - Activities and materials include the description of a democratic society with the concepts of liberty, justice, equality, and the rule of law; rights and responsibilities of individuals; and the "common good" for all of society. Typical early investigations for young children begin with the rules of the classroom—living in the school together—and expand through the appropriate exploration of historical and current events. (National Council for Social Studies, 1994)

The strategies for instruction within a classroom include individual investigations, small-group collaboration, and large-group discussions. Thus, the environment created must be a spatial layout that supports all of these strategies. In thinking about the space, it may be useful to refer to the classroom baseline—this includes not only the room arrangement, but also the schedule and the contents of the bulletin board, learning centers, and classroom resources arrayed for child discovery.

- *Room arrangement*—traffic patterns match the classroom activities planned. Learning centers are clearly set up and defined by topic with appropriate space to match the activities. Equipment and materials are accessible and grouped to encourage child management of them.

- *Schedule*—reflects a balance of individual, small-group, and large-group activity structure. A well-developed schedule includes large blocks of time during the week to support theme-based curricular endeavors. (Berry & Mindes, 1993)

The way that classroom space is used clearly shows the values and culture of the school or community (Gandini, 1998). A warm and welcoming social studies classroom will have posters displaying child questions, results of data gathered, pictures, structural products that document learning, and comfortable spaces for both individual and small-group work. The classroom may contain materials passed from one group of children to another, for example, our book on the trip to the fire station. This book then becomes a part of the cultural history of children and a resource for the class. As well, the space will display materials that families contribute to the ongoing projects and contain references to field trips made as part of the social studies investigations. Such materials pertain to the themes investigated, so there may be pictures of locations, such as the grocery store or apple orchard, and events, such as a family celebration of Kwanza or Diwali.

The environment will pay attention to the following elements:

Connections and a sense of belonging

- Pictures of children at work or pictures from home showing families.

Flexible space and open-ended materials

- Tables and chairs grouped in circles, in pods, or individually, as the activities dictate. Blocks, paints, construction paper, paper of all kinds, markers, crayons, etc.

Natural materials that engage the senses

- Fall leaves, stones, fruits, and vegetables.

Wonder, curiosity, and intellectual engagement

- Magnifying glasses to examine butterflies or the particles in a brick.

Symbolic representations, literacy, and the visual arts

- Books, calculators, computers, telephones, maps, charts, easels, clay, etc. (Curtis & Carter, 2003, p. 14)

Children receive messages from the environment that tell each child that they will be safe and comfortable

- Room dividers and shelves at eye level; both teacher and child can see everywhere.
- Space to move around
- Furniture is child-sized, solid, and well-maintained
- Room is clean and neat

In the right place and valued

- Pictures reflect community and families
- Display space for children's work
- Diversity of learners is represented

Able to share and develop friendships

- Cooperative activity is supported with small table structures
- Materials are grouped for sharing
- Message board for children and families

Knowledgeable of clear expectations

- Materials within reach
- Schedule is posted at child's eye level
- Labels for activities and materials are abundant
- Job responsibilities are posted

Doing work that is interesting

- Room is attractive and inviting
- Sufficient quantities of books and materials
- Variety of writing tools
- Displays change regularly. (Bickart, Jablon, & Dodge, 1999, pp. 100–101)

Effective social studies classrooms will contain the following elements: meeting area, display space, storage for personal belongings and ongoing work, classroom library, storage space for paper and tools for writing, homemade games, art and construction materials, blocks of all sizes, props and accessories, cooking materials and equipment, music, dance and drama, computer area with Internet access, and quiet spaces (Bickart et al., 1999).

The displays are as important as the furniture arrangement. Displays should entice the learner to explore new concepts, document learning accomplishments, and communicate the values of the classroom. Questions to ask when adding material to the walls:

- What is the purpose of the material—for the children, families, visitors?

- What image of learning do the materials convey?
- Does the display honor children's work or merely serve as decoration?
- Do posters and other displayed artifacts invite child participation?
- How do the materials contribute to a learning classroom atmosphere in the room?
- What are the assumptions about learning reflected by the classroom walls? (Tarr, 2004)

Besides furniture and displays, well-developed classrooms pay attention to the ambience of light, color, texture, and noise. Space for privacy is available and there are areas organized according to the need for space for the task. Social density, that is, small spaces for children at work individually, in small groups, or in class meetings are comforting to children. However, rooms with insufficient space for activities lead to disorder and, often, inappropriate behavior (Jalongo & Isenberg, 2004, pp. 152–163). As well, classrooms are flexible.

Design principles for effective learning include the following:

- Define the areas
- Provide more space for areas that will have blocks, manipulatives, and dramatic play
- Separate noisy from quiet areas
- Include space for solitary activity and small groups
- Consider the pathways between areas—wide enough and clear enough, but not runways for running. (Feeney, Christensen, Moravcik, 2006, pp. 226–228)

Also, check the room to be sure that classroom space meets the needs for young children with an environment that supports the following:

- Personal care routines relating to health, comfort, and safety
- Development with available storage, appropriate furniture, and display space
- Language–reasoning experiences with materials, interactions, experiences for discussion, and exploration
- Fine and gross motor activities
- Creative activities

- Social development with space for interactions
- Adult needs for record keeping and conferencing. (Henniger, 2005, p. 223)

*Learning centers* that support social studies will vary according to the age of children in the room, but some basic considerations for the span of years include art center, book center, and music center. At kindergarten, well-designed environments will include a dramatic play center, writing, and manipulatives center. You may see as well centers for woodworking and sand/water. By first grade and throughout the primary years, centers include math, science, and social studies centers supported by *prop boxes*— those materials gathered to support the theme in whole or part. Examples include boxes of materials related to a grocery store, bus station, bank, grandparents, office, or medical personnel.

Another consideration for learning center development is the need to have sufficient materials. A rule of thumb for twenty children is seventy choices of materials so that children will be actively engaged in center-based learning (Feeney et al., 2006, p. 234). In addition, when monitoring centers, avoid clutter, introduce new materials, rotate materials on the shelves, remove damaged items, and model respect for materials by mending, cleaning, or refurbishing (Feeney et al., 2006, pp. 234–235).

Centers must promote:

- Integration of learning across the developmental domains— cognitive, social–emotional, physical
- Enthusiastic participation for using the materials
- Sustained interest for the tasks or discovery opportunities
- Curiosity and perseverance for sustained learning
- Expression and expansion of various conceptual understandings
- Both convergent and divergent learning opportunities
- Sufficient materials for use at diverse levels of complexity. (Kostelnik, Soderman, & Whiren, 2004)

### Toys, Texts, Literature, Symbols, and Classroom Equipment in the Lives of Young Children

As you implement the broad social studies themes, the baseline of the room shifts to accommodate the focus. Thus, the bulletin board may contain pictures of family members as you study "families." The learning centers contain replica cars, trucks, and trains to support the study of "transportation." The classroom library contains books on Chicago or

New York, to support a study of "neighborhood" or community. In this way, the classroom environment evolves and stays engaging for young children.

As well, there are constants in the room that are adaptable to the study of diverse topics. These materials include blocks, paints, paper, props to support dramatic play, supplies for writing, and materials for constructing exhibits, sewing materials, woodworking materials, as well as clay or other modeling materials. These are the open-ended materials that offer many possibilities for children to explore along with their increasing understanding of the social studies topic.

*Children's literature* serves as the backbone for enrichment of child knowledge. "Reading literature involves a dimension beyond reading ordinary material. If read properly, a classic tale draws out a feeling of wholeness or oneness, a carefully drawn character or situation evokes a feeling of recognition, and a poem that speaks to the heart engenders a feeling of tranquility" (Gunning, 2005, p. 410). Thus, the human dilemmas of the past and present become accessible to young children as they read or hear folklore, poetry, chapter books, drama, and novels. The following list presents examples of books that lend themselves to the development of literacy as well as to the enhancement of social studies themes.

Barton, B. (1973). *Buzz, buzz, buzz.* New York: Macmillan.
Brown, M. (1996). *Stone soup.* Weston, CT: Weston Woods.
Carle, E. (1970). *The very hungry caterpillar.* New York: World Publishing.
Crews, D. (1978). *Freight train.* New York: World Publishing.
Martin, B. (1989). *Chicka, chicka boom boom.* New York: Simon & Schuster.
Most, B. (1990). *The cow that went oink.* San Diego: Harcourt.
Sendak, M. (1988). *Where the wild things are.* New York: Harper & Row.
Zelinsky, P. (1990). *The wheels on the bus.* New York: Dutton.

In addition to the choices of fictional books that are evocative of feelings and attitudes, children can access the issues and topics of social studies through children's nonfiction—biographies, informational books such as concept books, life-cycle books, experiment and activity books, books derived from original documents and journals, and photographic essays (Stoodt-Hill & Amspaugh-Corson, 2005, pp. 200–204). In selecting among the many informational books available to support the social studies, Stoodt-Hill and Amspaugh-Corson (2005, pp. 204–207) suggest that you consider the following factors and choose those with

- Thought-provoking text
- Style—use of language or voice

- Technique that hooks the reader
- Authority in the subject or a supportive panel of experts
- Accuracy
- Appropriateness for your learners
- Attractiveness

The National Council for Social Studies (www.ncss.org) annually publishes lists of notable books that support social studies topics. Biographies form a natural link to children's creation of biographies based on interviews and collected oral histories. To select relevant books for your thematic purpose, collect books that offer diverse perspectives and varying reading levels. In addition to children's literature, the social studies curriculum lends itself to introducing children to a variety of reference sources.

*Reference materials* facilitate child investigation skills. Such materials include newspapers and magazines. These resources are particularly important when thinking about current topics. Some examples of these materials are *Time for Kids* (http://www.timeforkids.com/TFK), *My Weekly Reader*, *Let's Find Out*, and *Scholastic News*. Additional reference materials are dictionaries, videotapes of TV news about the community, audiotapes of historically important speeches, and calendars (Seefeldt, 2005, pp. 105–106). Besides print media, you will want to include a variety of other reference material to use for investigating the social studies.

*Maps and globes* are important equipment for social studies. *Mapmaking* is an activity that involves child production of a map (Welton, 2005, p. 332). Welton suggests that mapmaking is a precursor to the understanding and use of maps. He suggests that young children begin with the bird's-eye view of objects that they map and advance to documentation of their environment, for example, the classroom, their backyard, the playground. Mapmaking involves using symbols, lines, and color to make representational pictures of the child's world. The activity also involves scale, that is, representing a large space on a small piece of paper. To prepare children for using scale, rulers, and other traditional mapmaking tools, you may wish to develop block structures to represent a "view" of what they will map (Seefeldt & Galper, 2006). Thus, maps serve as both a reference source for instruction and a documentation of learning. You will want to be sure that your room includes many examples and that you use various formats for summarizing information.

Maps in the classroom include relief maps, computer-based maps, satellite maps, wall maps, floor maps, weather maps, and globes. Try to find maps with lots of symbols that show your community, neighborhood, and state. Tourist maps, chamber of commerce maps, local transportation agencies, rental car companies, and walking guides are good sources for these materials (Seefeldt & Galper, 2006). Maps support the basic geography standards that organize geographical understanding around five themes: the world in spatial terms, places and regions, physical systems, human systems, and environment and society (Joint Committee on Geographic Education, 1984). In addition to maps, social studies data are summarized by using many popular pictorial methods.

*Graphs*, *tables*, and *charts* are the tools that children use for summarizing the results of their research. Time lines, including photographic time lines, facilitate children's ability to see events in perspective. Besides the books, specialized reference materials, and data-gathering summary techniques, there are two other ways that children learn about the social studies— through guest speakers and field trips.

*Guest speakers* make social studies current and lively. If you invite guests, you will need to talk with them before they appear at the classroom door so that the goals for the presentation will meet the needs of your class. Ask them to bring visual aids, which may include photos, charts, maps, pottery, jewelry, or other cultural artifacts. In addition, be sure to prepare children for the experience. Help them identify questions to ask the speaker and to remember ways to appreciate guest speakers with their attention, appropriate applause, and individual or group thank-you notes written after the event.

*Field trips* to the neighborhood or cultural, governmental, or business locations are an integral part of social studies education. They require preparation beforehand and careful organization for the event itself. See the following for a checklist of what to do to prepare for these events.

The trip is clearly linked to a curricular objective.

Visit the location first and make plans for the children's experience.

Secure parents' permission.

Gather volunteers, one for every two to four children, depending on age.

Prepare the children for the trip with stories, props, video clips, and pictures.

Review trip safety rules.

Prepare trip ID badges without child names, so you and the children can recognize each other, but a stranger won't use the child's name inappropriately.

Develop and follow a map, one for each group.

Help children see the items or activities so they can link the experience to the curriculum.

Give clipboards to children to complete graphing or other assignments.

Take pictures. (Seefeldt, 2005)

In addition, with an Internet connection, there are many possible virtual field trips—Abraham Lincoln's home, the White House, Colonial Williamsburg, etc. The virtual field trip is just one way that multimedia supports the social studies. An ever-increasing volume of multimedia materials offer research and literacy development opportunities for young children as well as a powerful mirror for our society.

### Examination of Video, Computer Instruction and Mass Media, and the Changing Nature of School

Multimedia supports for social studies include audiotapes, books on tape, DVDs, live TV, computers with access to the Internet, and computer software. One medium that has become ubiquitous in classrooms across the nation is the computer that serves both as tool and cognitive modifier. The National Association for the Education of Young Children (NAEYC, 1996) developed guidelines for computers in the classroom. Caveats are that teachers must judge to ensure

- age-appropriate, individually appropriate, and culturally appropriate software and Internet site,
- cognitive, problem-solving, and social skill stimulation,
- integration of the technology into the whole of the curriculum, and
- equitable access for all children.

In addition, according to NAEYC guidelines (1996), computers should be set at appropriate heights for child use, have two chairs per setup to encourage social interaction, teacher visibility while children use the Internet, and activities throughout the day so that the computer functions to enhance cognition in many ways. As well as the NAEYC guidelines, you will want to address the International Society for Technology in Education (ISTE) standards, which include content and processes for computing in the curriculum.

The ISTE standards for technology for all children focus on the development of the knowledge, skills, and attitudes for

- basic operations and concepts,
- social, ethical, and human issues,
- technology communication tools,
- technology production tools,
- technology research tools, and
- technology problem-solving and research tools.

For children up to Grade 2, these applications look like instruction that promotes child use of computers, VCRs, DVD player, audio recording devices, the Internet, and software (ISTE, 1998). These standards are particularly applicable to the social studies curriculum, since one of the primary goals for instruction is facilitation of problem-solving and research skills. Instruction supports an "appreciation for the use of technology to understand, control, and change the world throughout history; use of tools for design; and learn about technological equipment" (Bickart et al., 1999, p. 406). A natural way to integrate the computer into the classroom is to model its use as a communication vehicle. Following is a list of examples of the kinds of software and Web sites to use in preschool/primary settings. (A version of this list originally appeared in *Young Children*, September.)

### Web Sites

A&E Classroom, http://www.aetv.com.

American Presidents: Life Portraits, http://www.americanpresidents. org.

Asia Source, http://askasia.org.

Awesome Library, http://www.awesomelibrary.org.

Brave Girls and Strong Women, http://members.aol.com/brvgirls/ bklist.htm#.

Busy Teachers' Network, http://www.ceismc.gatech.edu/busyt/.

Carol Otis Hurst, Author of Numerous Books and Articles on Children's Literature, http://www.carolhurst.com.

Center for Economic Education, http://ecedweb.unomaha.edu.

Center on Congress at Indiana University, http://congress.indiana.edu.

Center for Media Literacy, http://www.medialit.org.

Character Development, http://www.cetac.org.

Children's Book Council, http://cbcbooks.org.

Children's Software Review, http://www.childrenssoftware.com.

Consumer Reports for Children, http://www.zillions.org.

Eduhound: Everything for the K-12 Educator, http://www. EduHound.com.

enVision Your World, http://www.envisionyourworld.com.

epals Classroom Exchange, http://www.epals.com/.

Geography Network, http://www.geographynetwork.com.

History Channel, http://www.historychannel.com.

Horn Book, http://www.hbook.com.

IT & Society, http://www.IT&Society.org.

Kathy Schrock's Guide to Education, http://school.discovery.com/ schrockguide/.

Kids Bank, http://www.kidsbank.com.

Kids Web-Japan, http://web-japan.org/kidsweb/.

Learning Page, http://www.learningpage.com.

Library of Congress, http://marvel.loc.gov/homepage/lchp.html.

MarcoPolo. Social studies and language arts integrated. http://www. marcopolo-education.org.

Miami University Children's Literature Database, http://www.lib. muohio.edu/pictbks.

Memorial Day History, http://www.usmemorialday.org.

National Council for the Social Studies, http://www.ncss.org.

National Gallery of Art, http://www.nga.gov.

National Geographic, http://nationalgeographic.com.

National Public Radio, http://www.justicelearning.org.

NetSmartz Workshop, http://netsmartz.org.

Oyate, http://www.oyate.org.

Personalizing Data with Digital Portfolios, http://www.ascd.org/ pub-lications/class_lead/200303/niguidula_3.html.

Pilgrims, http://www.pilgrims.net/plimothplantation.

Public Broadcasting System, http://pbs.org/teachersource.

Rand McNally K 12 Online, http://www.k12online.com.

ReadWriteThink. Standards based teaching, http://www.readwritethink.org.

RepeatAfterUs.com, http://repeatafterus.com.

Scholastic for Teachers, http://teacher.scholastic.com.

Scholastic Resource for Choosing Scholastic Books by Topic/Grade, http://teacher.scholastic.com/teachingstrategies/.

Small Planet Communications, http://www.smplanet.com.

Smithsonian Museum, http://www.si.edu.

Social Studies for Kids, http://www.socialstudiesforkids.com.

SuperKids Educational Software, http://superkids.com.

Teaching Tolerance, an Internet resource of the Southern Poverty Law Center, http://www.tolerance.org.

tech.Learning, http://www.techlearning.com.

Topographic Maps, http://topozone.com.

USA Today, http://www.usatoday.com/educate/home.htm.

US Bureau of the Census, http://www.census.gov.

US Citizenship and Immigration Services, http://uscis.gov/graphics/aboutus/history/teacher/index.htm.

US Congress, http://www.congresslink.org.

US Department of Education, http://www.ed.gov.

US Department of Justice, http://www.cbercrime.gov/rules/kidinternet.htm.

US Department of Labor, http://www.dol.gov.

US Geological Survey, http://www.usgs.gov.

Kay Vandergrift at Rutgers University, http://www.scils.rutgers.edu/~kvander/ChildrenLit/index.html.

World Almanac for Kids, http://www.worldalmanacforkids.com/index.html.

## Software

Graph Club 2.0. New York: Tom Snyder.

Kidpix Deluxe 3.0. San Francisco: Learning Company.

Kidspiration. Portland, OR: Inspiration.

If the World Were a Village. New York: Tom Snyder.

Neighborhood Map Machine 2.0. New York: Tom Snyder.

Oregon Trail 5th ed. San Francisco: Learning Company.

Timeliner 5.0. New York: Tom Snyder.

USA Explorer Teacher Pack. New York: Scholastic.

## DVDs examples from the Public Broadcasting website http://www.pbs.org

Arthur and the Scare Your Pants off Club

A Nation of Many Colors

American Flag

Don't Forget to Write

Family Tales

Homes Sweet Homes

I Have a Dream

Neighborhood Helpers

Tall Sturdy Building

Travel: For Younger Students

Wayback Family Ties

One use of the computer connection is to provide opportunities for family and teacher connections through class homepages and email contacts. The homepage can feature

- calendar of classroom events,
- parenting information,
- homework and grading policies, and
- home learning opportunities. (Charland, 1998)

In addition, you will want to include appropriate software for the classroom to facilitate knowledge and skill acquisition.

Thus, when selecting software, you will want to include a certain number of interactive software programs that are drill- and practice-based. These will support learning for children who may require extra practice.

Basic categories for software support learning across the curriculum. Guidelines for selecting software:

- Storyboard—interactive templates for story creation by children
- Draw/paint—interactive templates for drawing, creating art
- Electronic books—computer reading to children

- Writing/publishing software—interactive templates that support child writing and illustrations. (Henniger, 2005)

In addition to thinking about classroom software, you will need to consider access to multimedia for all of your learners.

## Issues of Equity and Power Related to Media

A number of studies and reports document that a *digital divide* exists in the United States. Digital divide is a gap between higher-income and lower-income groups in terms of access to technology. Most of the documentation of this topic comes from the approach that examines computer access from home. However, Robinson, DiMaggio, and Hargittai (2003) provide evidence that digital divide varies by parents' education and occasionally by income, age, and marital status. Thus, college-educated families have the digital advantage. In examining the problem, Robinson et al. show that *information access*, also known as a "knowledge gap" is the historical divide that continues to the present. Evidence of this information access divide were presented in the "Cincinnati Experiment" in 1947, which sought with a six-month multimedia campaign to inform the public about the United Nations. The study by Hyman and Sheatsley in 1950 (in Robinson et al., 2003, p. 2) showed that those who were already informed learned more, but the uninformed remained the have-nots.

> A more recent and familiar example concerns the highly popular TV program, *Sesame Street*, created to reduce the gap in preschool children's academic ability and skills using the power of public television to reach all segments of the population. Once again, however, watching *Sesame Street*, was found to increase the preschool knowledge of middle-class children more than that of the working-class children it was intended to help. (Cook et al., 1975, in Robinson et al., 2003, pp. 2–3)

As teachers, you will try to develop multimedia literacy with the social studies curriculum to minimize the digital divide. For, "*media literacy* is a 21st century approach to education. It provides a framework to access, analyze, evaluate, and create messages in a variety of forms—from print to video to the Internet. Media literacy builds an understanding of the role of media in society as well as essential skills of inquiry and self-expression necessary for citizens of a democracy" (Center for Media Literacy, 2005, http://www.medialit.org). Nowhere in the curriculum are the issues of media literacy more inextricably linked to content and process goals for learning than in the social studies.

*Nonfiction trade books and fiction books* can frequently be used to support social studies themes. Suppose you are developing a theme about families. You might include the following books in your literacy center: *Dumpling Soup* (Rattigan, 1992), *Families Are Different* (Pellegrini, 1991), *The Grandpa Days* (Blos, 1989), *On the Day I Was Born* (Chocolate, 1995), *Who's in a Family?* (Skutch, 1995) *Fiesta* (Ancona, 1995). These books are in addition to *Kids Road Atlas* (n.d.), dictionaries, and encyclopedias. For sources to include in your classroom library, meet with your librarian; check *Hornbook* (http://Carolhurst.com) and the National Council for Social Studies annual list of "Notable Trade Books" to select materials for theme-based teaching as well as the other Web sites and guides listed at the end of this chapter.

*Textbooks* often are a feature of the primary social studies curriculum. They are convenient and contain information developed by experts. Children who read the text get the same information about a topic. To use textbooks effectively,

- give a purposeful reading assignment with the certainty that the learners can accomplish the task,
- stimulate interest in the reading by asking questions, telling incomplete stories, and giving thumbnail sketches of the material,
- provide assistance to individuals who need help, and
- follow up the reading by using it as part of the instruction. (Turner, 2004, p. 74)

To facilitate textbook reading, teach children the tools that successful readers use. These skills involve

Recognition of the organization of the materials
- Boldface headings as cues for content organization
- Topic sentences that can be used when skimming the material for overview
- Identification of the main idea and supporting details of paragraphs or passages

Bringing meaning to the reading
- By learning the vocabulary and concepts through direct experiential activities
- Using glossaries and dictionaries to find meanings
- Relating to personal experiences
- Recognizing sequencing devices used by authors

Reading for purpose

- Setting up the purpose with questions and problems
- Skimming for overall meaning
- Scanning for specific information
- Using the index and table of contents to find specific ideas
- Using the maps, illustrations, charts, and graphs to support understanding of the text

Read critically

- Recognizing author bias
- Recognizing discrepancies, contradictions, missing information
- Identifying relationships among the elements, for example, cause and effect, sequencing
- Distinguishing opinion from fact and description from interpretation. (Turner, 2004, pp. 75–76)

The single most important aspect for facilitating comprehension in reading is to be sure that children have the vocabulary to read the material (Shanahan, 2001). Direct teaching of vocabulary as part of making the textbook accessible to young children is effective when

- only words central to understanding are taught,
- words are taught in context,
- prior knowledge is used to connect the new words,
- words are taught in the rich context of the theme under study, and
- there are many exposures to the word. (Cooper & Kiger, 2006)

Additional strategies for learning words from context consist of the following:

- Read the whole sentence and decide whether the word is critical to understanding; if not, ignore it.
- Look for base words, prefixes, and suffixes you recognize, if the word is important.
- Reread and try to derive the meaning from context.
- Reread when you think you know the meaning to be sure that it makes sense. (Cooper & Kiger, 2006)

Other techniques that assist students in learning vocabulary are word maps, semantic feature analysis grids, Venn diagrams, and other graphic organizers. Figure 6.1 illustrates graphic organizers.

In using any text materials, be wary of those books that have few words and many ideas compacted within. "The extent to which any passage contains ideas that are packed densely, sparsely, or somewhere in between is called *concept loading.* Concept load contributes to the material's *readability,* which is the relative ease or difficulty of reading and gaining meaning from material. Passages in which ideas are densely packed, and thus have a high concept load, are usually more difficult to understand than passages with a lower concept load" (Welton, 2005, p. 183). Other issues with textbooks include the need to be sure that children can understand the specialized vocabulary from the text and that definitions support figurative and abstract concepts.

Textbooks can provide background information on a topic, serve as a source to verify hypotheses that arise in class discussion, and provide definitions and illustrations that pertain to the topic (Welton, 2005,

**Figure 6.1**
**Examples of Graphic Organizers to Facilitate Organized Learning**

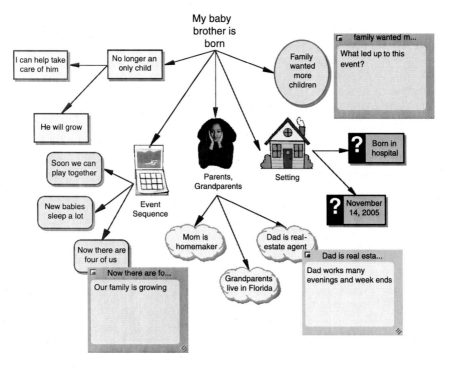

**Figure 6.1
(Continued)**

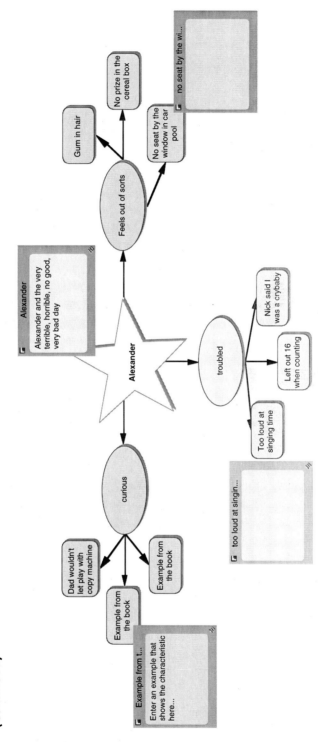

**Figure 6.1
(Continued)**

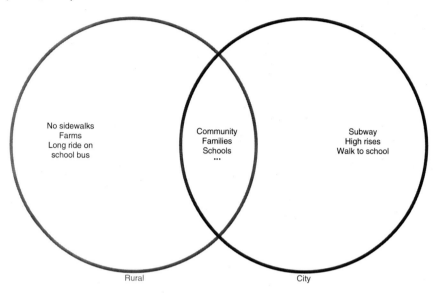

All graphics prepared with Inspiration as examples.

pp. 357–358). So, if you are going to use textbooks, consider when and how the textbook will support the learning objectives. It is unnecessary to read the book from page one to the end; select the parts that meet your goals. Duplass (2004) recommends the following guidelines when using textbooks:

Using a scale to evaluate the text, ask

- What is the figurative or literal meaning?
- Is it accurate or inaccurate?
- To what degree is the information biased or objective?
- Are there inferred as well as explicit messages?
- Is the message by the author subtle or obvious?
- Is there both cognitive and affective appeal? (p. 153)

In selecting which parts of the book to read, ask

- Can any procedural knowledge be developed with the content?
- Can a Big Idea be developed?
- Can other materials be used to bring the content to life?

- Can the content be made relevant to students' lives? (p. 162)

In selecting materials to read for point of view, ask if
- a variety of cultures is found in illustrations and photos,
- a variety of cultures is found in the writing,
- a stereotype is presented; for example, all the women are home cooking,
- various cultural groups are represented by the main characters, and
- material is written by people from various cultures.

Besides textbooks, the most often chosen material for social studies instruction is children's literature, as discussed earlier in this chapter.

## Summary

This chapter focused on setting up the room for optimum social studies learning. Then, the focus turned to selection of materials to support social studies instruction. First, there were social studies experiences within the regular schedule. Then, there was a focus on how to incorporate children's literature and trade books in the social studies themes. Also included was a discussion of the possible role of textbooks with guidelines for their selection, since these are often part of the required curriculum of public school primary grades. Multimedia, their use, limitations, and access featured a discussion of the changing societal notions regarding technology.

## Activities in the Field

1. Visit classrooms at different age/grade levels. Sketch the room organization. Do the rooms meet the guidelines discussed above?
2. Interview children to ask about their use of media. Which do they use at school? At home? How does this compare with your childhood experiences?
3. Watch a television program aimed toward teaching young children about a social studies topic. Would the program be of value to the early childhood social studies curriculum?

## Activities in the Library

1. Visit the Web sites suggested in this chapter. How would you use them to teach a particular concept or topic?

2. Review several child textbooks written for primary-age children. Do they match the criteria discussed in this chapter?

3. Look at the child reference books available in your library. How do these support the social studies?

## Study Questions

1. What role does the classroom environment play in the curriculum?

2. How do learning centers support instruction in social studies?

3. How do you use textbooks and the specialized materials of the social studies?

4. What role does children's literature—both fiction and nonfiction—play in supporting the social studies?

5. When and how do you use multimedia in the social studies curriculum?

## Reflect and Re-read

1. Think about the relationship of environment to instructional method and philosophical values.

2. Compare the issues of bias in society with instructional methodology and materials. In which ways will you keep the principles of human dignity and respect at the forefront as you develop curricula?

## Suggested Readings

Chalufour, I., & Worth, K. (2004). *Building structures with young children.* St. Paul: Red Leaf Press. Written as one of a series on science education for young children, this practical book has much to offer in terms of practical advice on forms of structures and activities to facilitate building activities.

Curtis, D., & Carter, M. (2003). *Designs for living and learning: Transforming early childhood environments.* St. Paul: Red Leaf Press. With this book, the authors offer a thought-provoking challenge to the way in which we have come to set up classrooms. Throughout the eight chapters, the authors illustrate with words and glorious full-color pictures how to set up classrooms that are not humdrum.

Diffily, D., & Sassman, C. (2002). *Project-based learning with young children.* Portsmouth, NH: Heinemann. Practical suggestions for implementation of this approach to learning, with sample topics, schedules, and storage ideas.

Heroman, C., & Jones, C. (2004). *Literacy: The creative curriculum approach.* Washington, DC: Teaching Strategies. Activities and books for use in the learning centers of the classroom.

Kristo, J. V., & Bamford, R. A. (2004). *Nonfiction in focus: A comprehensive framework for helping students become independent readers and writers of nonfiction, K-6.* New York: Scholastic. Suggestions for the selection of nonfiction materials and helpful checklists and sources.

Wyman, R. M. (2005). *America's history through young voices: Using primary sources in the K-12 social studies classroom.* Boston: Allyn & Bacon. This book provides suggestions and activities for using "stories" to support social studies topics in American history.

# References

Berry, C. F., & Mindes, G. (1993). *Planning a theme-based curriculum: Goals, themes, activities, and planning guides for 4's and 5's.* Glenview, IL: Good Year.

Bickart, T. S., Jablon, J. R., & Dodge, D. T. (1999). *Building the primary classroom: A comprehensive guide to teaching and learning.* Washington, DC: Teaching Strategies.

Center for Media Literacy. (2005). *Definition of media literacy.* Santa Monica: Author. Available from http://www.medialit.org/.

Charland, T. (1998). Classroom homepage connections. *T.H.E. Journal, 25*(9), 62–64.

Cook, T. D., et al. (1975). *Sesame Street revisited.* New York: Russell Sage. In Robinson, J. P., DiMaggio, P., & Hargittai, E. (2003). New social survey perspectives on the digital divide. *IT & Society, 1*(5), 1–22.

Cooper, J. D., & Kiger, N. D. (2006). *Literacy: Helping children construct meaning* (6th ed.). Boston: Houghton Mifflin.

Curtis, D., & Carter, M. (2003). *Designs for living and learning: Transforming early childhood environments.* St. Paul: Red Leaf Press.

Duplass, J. A. (2004). *Teaching elementary social studies: What every teacher should know.* Boston: Houghton-Mifflin.

Feeney, S., Christensen, D., & Moravcik, E. (2006). *Who am I in the lives of children?* (7th ed.). Upper Saddle River, NJ: Prentice-Hall/Merrill.

Gandini, L. (1998). Educational and caring spaces. In C. Edwards, L. Gandini, & G. Forman (Eds.), *The hundred languages of children: The Reggio Emilia approach—advanced reflections* (2nd ed., pp. 161–178). Greenwich, CT: Ablex.

Gunning, T. G. (2005). *Creating literacy: Instruction for all students* (5th ed.). Boston: Allyn & Bacon.

Henniger, M. L. (2005). *Teaching young children* (3rd ed.). Upper Saddle River, NJ: Prentice-Hall/Merrill.

Hyman, H. H., & Sheatsley, P. B. (1950). The current status of American public opinion. In J. C. Payne (Ed.), *The teaching of contemporary affairs* (pp. 11–34). New York: National Education Association. In Robinson, J. P., DiMaggio, P., & Hargittai, E. (2003). New social survey perspectives on the digital divide. *IT & Society, 1*(5), 1–22. Available from http://www.IT&society.org.

International Society for Technology Education. (1998). *National educational technology standards for students.* Eugene, OR: Author.

Jalongo, M. R., & Isenberg, J. P. (2004). *Exploring your role: A practitioner's introduction to early childhood education.* (2nd ed.). Upper Saddle River, NJ: Prentice-Hall/Merrill.

Joint Committee on Geographic Education. (1984). *Guidelines for geographic education.* Washington, DC: National Council for Geographic Education and the Association of American Geographers.

Kostelnik, M. J., Soderman, A. K., & Whiren, A. P. (2004). *Developmentally appropriate curriculum: Best practices in early childhood education* (3rd ed.). Upper Saddle River, NJ: Prentice-Hall/Merrill.

National Association for Young Children. (1996). NAEYC position statement: Technology and young children—ages three through eight. *Young Children, 51*(6), 11–16.

National Council for Social Studies. (1994). *Expectations for excellence: Curriculum standards for social studies.* Washington, DC: Author.

Robinson, J. P., DiMaggio, P., & Hargittai, E. (2003). New social survey perspectives on the digital divide. *IT & Society, 1*(5), 1–22.

Seefeldt, C. (2005). *Social studies for the preschool/primary child* (7th ed.). Upper Saddle River, NJ: Prentice-Hall/Merrill.

Seefeldt, C., & Galper, A. (2006). *Active experiences for active children: Social studies* (2nd ed.). Upper Saddle River, NJ: Prentice-Hall/Merrill.

Shanahan, T. (2001). *The notational reading panel: Teaching children to read* (Chapter 4). Newark, DE: International Reading Association. Available from www.reading.org.advocacy//nrp/chapter4.html.

Stoodt-Hill, B. D., & Amspaugh-Corson, L. B. (2005). *Children's literature: Discovery for a lifetime* (3rd ed.). Upper Saddle River, NJ: Prentice-Hill/Merrill.

Tarr, P. (2004). Consider the walls. *Beyond the journal: Young children on the web.* Available from www.naeyc.org.

Turner, T. N. (2004). *Essentials of elementary social studies* (3rd ed.). Boston: Allyn & Bacon.

Welton, D. (2005). *Children and their world: Strategies for teaching social studies* (8th ed.). Boston: Houghton Mifflin.

## Children's Literature

Ancona, G. (1995). *Fiesta.* New York: Lodestar.

Blos, J. W. (1989). *The grandpa days.* New York: Simon & Schuster.

Chocolate, D. (1995). *On the day I was born.* New York: Scholastic.

*Kids Road Atlas.* (n.d.). Skokie, IL: Rand McNally.

Pellegrini, N. (1991). *Families are different.* New York: Holiday House.

Rattigan, J. K. (1992). *Dumpling soup.* Boston: Joy Street Books.

Skutch, R. (1995). *Who's in the family?* Berkeley: Tricycle Press.

## Web Sites

Carol Otis Hurst: http://www.carolhurst.com. Author of numerous books and articles on children's literature.

Children's Book Council: http://cbcbooks.org. This trade association for booksellers seeks to make reading pleasurable for children. The site contains information about newly published children's books.

Children's Software Review: http://www.childrenssoftware.com. Reviews of popular software for children to use at home and school.

Kay Vandergrift at Rutgers University: http://www.scils.rutgers.edu/~kvander/ChildrenLit/index.html. A resource for finding children's literature and activities for using the literature.

Library of Congress: http://marvel.loc.gov/homepage/lchp.html. The gateway to a rich federal resource for children, teachers, and families.

MarcoPolo. Social studies and language arts integrated: http://www.marcopolo-education.org. Lesson plans and unit topics.

Miami University Children's Literature Database: http://www.lib.muohio.edu/pictbks. Reviews of children's literature prepared by library science students.

National Council for the Social Studies: http://www.ncss.org. Practical discussions of lesson development as well as policy statements related to teaching social studies and an annual booklist released in May of each year.

National Gallery of Art: http://www.nga.gov. Programs, films, and art events for children.

National Geographic: http://nationalgeographic.com. Classroom activities, games and homework help for children.

The Netsmartz Workshop: http://www.netsmartz.org. An interactive Web site to teach Internet safety.

ReadWriteThink. Standards based teaching: http://www.readwritethink.org. Integrated teaching methods and project-based lesson plans.

Smithsonian Museum: http://www.si.edu. Special sections for teachers and children, including interactive Internet lessons.

U.S. Department of Justice: http://www.cbercrime.gov/rules/kidinternet.html. A guide for safe practices on the Internet and the gateway to other department of justice sites.

# CHAPTER 7

# Assessing the Accomplishment of Learning in the Social Studies

Nothing strengthens the judgment and quickens the conscience like individual responsibility. Nothing adds such dignity to character as the recognition of one's self-sovereignty; the right to an equal place, everywhere conceded—a place earned by personal merit, not an artificial attainment by inheritance, wealth, family and position. Elizabeth Cady Stanton (1815–1902), U.S. suffragist, social reformer, and author. *The Solitude of Self* (February 20, 1894)

## Terms to Know

- Assessment
- Benchmarks
- Standards
- Backward design
- Observation
- Curricular mapping
- Portfolios
- Performance assessment
- Formative
- Summative
- Multiple data source
- Anecdotal records

- Rating scales
- Rubrics
- Authentic assessment
- Checklists
- Questionnaires
- Criterion-referenced assessment
- Norm-referenced
- Mastery learning
- Stakeholders
- Align

## Overview

Teachers engage in assessment activities most often for instructional planning and to judge whether individuals and the class as a whole have met the objectives for the theme, unit, or year. Other reasons to assess young children include student placement and for accountability to diverse publics—children, parents, administrators, and community. Thus, *assessment* is a process of data gathering for the purpose of making judgments about student progress and deciding what to do next in the teaching–learning process. For the social studies, this means keeping track of not only the content of the field, but also the social skills that are an inherent part of the curriculum.

## Focus Questions

1. How do you decide what to teach, how much time to spend on the topic, and when it is learned? Where do the social studies fit?
2. When and how can you involve the children in choosing learning goals and assessing progress?
3. What role do parents play in the assessment process?
4. How do you demonstrate respect for the parental perspective?
5. Which assessment strategy can you use for getting the information that you need?
6. How do you incorporate standardized measures in the assessment process?
7. What do stakeholders want to know and how do you tell them?

## Using Assessment for Goal Setting

All classroom-based assessment begins with reflection on educational purpose. What is the goal for learning? What skills, attitudes, and values will be instilled? What does the learning look like? How will you know that children have accomplished the expectations? To begin, then, look at the ten social studies themes described by the National Council for the Social Studies (1994) and dicussed earlier. While the themes and *benchmarks*—descriptors of expected learning components related to a particular goal—described here begin with kindergarten, the themes are broad enough to provide inspiration for overall preschool goals as well. Use these benchmarks in combination with philosophical statements, overall child development aspirations, and particular curricular mandates from organizations, for example, Head Start, for the "big picture" of a teaching–learning agenda. Of course, in the primary years, you will derive classroom goals from state *standards*—statements written in behavioral terms with exemplars that delineate component parts of individual standards. These standards are still broad statements that you must translate for day-to-day instruction. Because of the emphasis on accountability, teachers today are often required to use state or national professional goals established by learned societies or by state governments to prescribe content for instruction in the primary grades.

Once you have reviewed the program philosophy, standards, and benchmarks, you have the end points for lessons from the curricular standpoint; the next step is to consider where the learners are with regard to the background knowledge and skills required to build new learning. This approach to instruction is called *backward design*. Choose the target goal or objective, specify the evidence required to accomplish the goal, plan the activities, and assess the progress of achievement (Wiggins & McTighe, 2001). The fundamental technique for gathering this information is *observation*, a planned, systematic look at the children in general and in particular as they perform in the classroom.

A practical way to gather all of the pieces is through a process called *curricular mapping*, a schematic representation of a theme or program. Table 7.1 shows an example of this summary approach for a theme on pioneers to be implemented in a third-grade classroom.

*Attention to individual differences* is an important aspect of the planning process. Through review of previous records, review of results of screening assessment conducted prior to enrollment, and initial observation of the children in your class, you have a "picture" of who they are as individuals. Who needs structure to sit in large-group activities? Who

**Table 7.1**
**Curriculum Mapping Template**

|  | September | October |
|---|---|---|
| State Standard | IL STATE GOAL 16: Understand events, trends, individuals, and movements shaping the history of Illinois, the United States, and other nations |  |
| Content | Pioneers of 1840 | Pioneers of 1890 |
| Skill/ benchmarks | Reading map, grids, timelines | Critical reading of stories about pioneer life |
| Exit outcomes | Students will identify critical map features. Students will create grids to chart information gained in the research phase. Students will develop accurate timelines for the period studied. | Students will identify the characteristics of pioneer life. Students will read and interpret stories against the pioneer characteristics. Students will judge the accuracy of pioneer stories. |
| Assessment | Draw posters, make maps of historical site Follow directions and create butter product Complete a four-square quilt Write or tell histories of grandparents; compare to pioneers. | Kitchen schematic is historically accurate for the period. Medicine kit is historically accurate. School day contains materials and instruction typical of the time Main points of horse versus machine are covered |
| Activities | Tour of historical site Butter making Quilting Collecting oral histories of grandparents/comparing to pioneers and current | Design pioneer kitchen Develop pioneer medicine cabinet Develop a school day to simulate one-room school Debate the issue of the horseless carriage |
| Technology | Oregon Trail 5 (age 9 and above) The Oregon Tail website: http://www.isu.edu/%7Etrinmich/Oregontrail.html Sacajawea: http://www.sacajaweahome.com/ | Pioneer Kitchen: http://www.execulink.com/~ecpmchin/kitchen.htm Pioneer Medicine: http://library.thinkquest.org/J001587/medicine.htm |
| Other essential questions | Can children compare the recent past, pioneers, and think about what might have been happening globally? |  |

*Source:* Jacobs (2004).

experiences fine motor difficulties? Whose speech is just a bit unclear? Who reads, writes, or computes at an advanced level? Who works in small groups easily? Who needs more structure in small-group activities? Who is learning English? With all of these pictures in mind, you plan activities and assessment procedures that will support the children with disabilities, the English language learners, and others with temporary (out with the chicken pox) or long-term special needs.

## Ways to Involve Children in Assessment

One of the ways to empower children in their own learning and to show them how to monitor their accomplishments is to design activities that have embedded assessment strategies. Activities that you can use to promote and document learning include

### *Posters*

- These documents developed by the teacher or students offer self-checking mechanisms for young children as they monitor their behavior, project work, or academic tasks.
  *Example:* Create with the children a poster that illustrates how state governments help us, or the following chart:

### *Stop and Think Behavior Chart*

| What should I think and do? |
| --- |
| 1. Stop and think. |
| 2. Are you going to make a good choice or a bad choice? |
| 3. What are your choices or steps? |
| 4. Do it! |
| 5. Good job! |
| *Source:* Reprinted from Knoff (2001). |

### *Stories*

- When children write or tell stories about a concept, you know not only whether they have the concept of story, but also whether they understand the concept.

*Example:* Children tell stories about how pioneer children used toys like jump ropes, jacks, and games like Red Rover, Red Rover.

## Captions

- Writing or dictating a caption for a cartoon or picture shows comprehension of the topic at-hand.
  *Example:* Babies Can Eat, Sleep and . . .

## Editorials

- Writing or dictating an editorial about a social issue shows a grasp of the complexity of a problem studied.
  *Example:* The Chicago Transit Authority should maintain the bus schedule so that people can go to work. In addition, the bus keeps our city from becoming polluted with car exhaust.

## Charts

- Making charts to show timelines of events and that illustrate sequence of events or issues; such charts offer opportunities for children to display their knowledge and understanding about the issue.
  *Example:* A sequence showing what happens to money when it goes to the bank.

## Maps

- Making maps to illustrate geographical understanding or using a map to describe understandings offers a concrete way to document child knowledge.
  *Example:* I can draw a map that shows how I get to school.

## Visual and Performing Arts

- Permitting students to create posters, murals, and plays to document knowledge offers a holistic approach to showing the accomplishment of learning goals.
  *Example:* A mural showing how people in our class work.

## Oral presentations

- Require children to organize their thoughts that show understandings without necessarily the requirement of writing in order to document learning.
  *Example:* I can tell you why it is important not to talk to strangers.

## Journals

- Give children the opportunity to reflect upon learning after the activity is over.
  *Example:* When we went to the pioneer house, I saw how tiny the rooms were, but I remembered that pioneers had few tools and materials to make houses.

## Letters and email

- Writing to real or fictional individuals about a concept or topic gives children an opportunity to show comprehension.
  *Example:* Dear Thomas Edison, if I were inventing the light bulb today, I would . . .

## Essays

- Offering children an opportunity to write point-of-view or position statements at the upper-primary level gives them a way to show comprehensive understanding of a topic.
  *Example:* We should have lettuce everyday in the school lunch room because . . .

## Discussion

- Through participation in small- and large-group focused conversations, debates, and dialogues about an issue or topic, you can see what children know and understand.
  *Example:* Our school would be a better place if we. . . .

## Questions

- Responses to both oral and written questions are often used to assess fact knowledge. Students can write these as well.
  *Example:* What medicines did pioneers use when they got sick?

### *PowerPoint Presentations*

- Children in the primary grades can begin to organize these kinds of presentations to document knowledge.
  *Example:* This chart shows how many people like to eat the three kinds of apples that we tasted.

All of these activities are holistic in orientation and reflect a constructivist approach to instruction. To use the activities as part of an assessment plan for a thematic study, you will need to think about the benchmarks that show successful accomplishment of assignment goals. To document learning, you will need to develop *rubrics*—descriptions of the criteria that show whether the product is adequate or whether the process has been accomplished. Usually a rubric gives descriptions for a range of accomplishment: not-at-all, adequately, exemplary. Children can be involved in the development of rubrics once they understand the process and their function.

## Rubric Development

In developing rubrics, the first step is to identify qualities for the product or process, cluster the attributes, think about the weight of the attributes, and refine the draft. Then the learner or the teacher uses the rubric to self-assess, peer-assess, or to assess all the children in a particular class. Rubrics make the performance expectations explicit for activities and thus form part of the backbone of *authentic assessment*—evaluation strategies that are similar or identical to those routinely performed by children. For example, children describe their families—who lives with them and identify the kinds of families—extended, nuclear, single-parent—within their community as part of the theme on "families." At the conclusion of the study, each child draws a representation of a family and can tell the teacher why the drawing is a family—demonstrating comprehension of the concept. This authentic assessment is often called *performance assessment*, a strategy that demands the learner show the evaluator that a learning task can be completed. For example, as part of the conclusion of a study of "grocery store," students could show the teacher which products belong in the categories of produce, canned goods, meats, etc.

*Performance assessment* includes criteria and rubrics for scoring a task. Used at the beginning of a theme, you can design a task to assess what children already know. For example, for a study of money, you might ask the following questions: What is your experience with money? Do you have a bank, banking account? Then, in a learning center, you could ask children to match coins, order them in terms of value, and identify which ones will be needed to purchase a box of cereal or loaf of bread, etc. The questions and the tasks should match the age of the children and the goals of the instruction. The rubric to accompany the learning center assignment might be as follows:

1. Coins are matched: with accuracy, with some mistakes, or not at all.
2. Coins are ordered: consecutively, with some mistakes, or not at all.
3. Purchases are shown: with appropriate coins, with some mistakes, or not at all.

These tasks are authentic, with a real purpose and audience. Performance assessment allows learners to show the integration of content and skills. Such tasks permit the learner to show disciplined inquiry. Thus, they must be designed with academic rigor, explicit standards, and scoring criteria. Ideally, such tasks include requirements for elaborate communication, display various levels of thinking, and call for reflection. These tasks are designed to include self- and peer assessment. As authentic measures, they permit the learner to be flexible in content, strategies, and products displayed or performed. Examples include acting out a play to show an understanding of pioneer life, conducting an election to demonstrate knowledge of voting, or writing a poem to illustrate comprehension of the concept of patriotism. As part of an overall system for assessment and at the beginning of the development for a yearly plan of instruction, you should consider authentic ways to summarize student learning. One method that permits the display of learning holistically is the *portfolio*— a purposeful collection of learning products organized to show learning progress.

*Portfolios* are used for a variety of purposes: working, collection of works in progress organized by the learner; or display, summative demonstration of accomplishment at the conclusion of a theme or the year. Whatever the purpose, the teacher or learner must first create the purpose of the collection of material and identify the required evidence to show learning. The learning products displayed must include the scoring rubrics. Finally, the portfolio must be organized. Thus, a portfolio is more than a laundry basket of materials collected periodically. The portfolio is a focused *selection* of products that show learning progress according to learning goals and objectives. Examples of materials to include in portfolios include self-portrait, work samples, anecdotal notes, curriculum checklists showing child progress, child reflections, and videos of group projects.

Besides child, teacher, and principal, another major *stakeholder* (one who has vested interest in the outcome of assessment) are parents who can view the portfolio to see how the integrated learning approach works as well as gather information about their child's knowledge, skills, and attitudes shown in the portfolio. Thus, parents are important partners through the assessment process.

## Parents as Part of the Assessment Process

At the beginning of the year or at the time of enrollment, parents contribute a valuable perspective about their child as a learner. Through interviews, questionnaires, or screening activities, teachers learn about the life of Arnold before second grade—he and his family have moved five times; and about Matilde, who began reading before kindergarten. As well, parent perspective helps the preschool teacher know that Glenn had limited experience with other children before enrolling in a program for three-year-olds. This background information helps you know what special needs the various children in your class may have. It helps you see the learners as people with familial, cultural backgrounds, and learning interests and styles. When developing the interview or questionnaire, you must know something about the people in your community and plan a sensitive, respectful way to approach parents.

*Respecting parent perspective* includes beginning a conversation about non–school-related tasks in order to develop a sense of the personal about the learners within your classroom. Some questions to consider include the following:

- What is unique about your family?
- Do you have a family hobby or special interest?
- What does your family do for fun?
- What activity, food, and/or event is the most motivating for your child?
- What do you like to read about?
- What is your favorite family movie?
- How would you like to be involved at school—in your child's classroom, the PTA, or committees?
- What are your goals for your child?
- How does our school schedule match your work schedule?
- What is the best time of the day for you to come to school for a brief visit? (Venn & Jahn, 2004, p. 185)

Once you begin the conversation, you can have some success at encouraging ongoing parent involvement in their child's learning. Such involvement promotes overall school success. Factors that encourage family involvement include the following:

Fulfillment of basic needs

Home-school communication

Recognition of family differences

Home-based focus

Schoolwide goals

Multiple methods of involvement

Recognition

Children as recruiters

Inclusion of significant adults

Collaboration among families

Child care provisions. (cf. Gestwicki, 2004)

Thus, if you pay attention to these issues related to families, you have begun on the right foot for a successful learning partnership in the best interests of the learners in your class. Whether you are setting goals with families, establishing goals for the year or involved in thinking through the day-to-day assessment issues, you need to select the process for assessment that *aligns*—matches method of assessment to purpose—with your curricular expectation.

## Choosing an Assessment Method to Fit the Purpose of Learning

Once you have identified or developed learning goals and objectives for a specified period—week, month, quarter, semester, year—and planned the activities to carry out these goals, you will need to select a method to assess progress for these goals. There are varieties of techniques that offer the potential for assessing and record keeping. Growing out of observation—the basic method for collecting information about children and learning in early childhood—are techniques that help you focus the observation, recording, and summarization for the assessment focus. These include the following:

*Anecdotal records* are brief notes of events that document a child's play preference, ability to focus in a large group, ability to work in a small group, etc. These notes should include the date, description of the context, and an objective recording of an individual child's behavior.

*Rating scales* require the assessor to judge the quality of the child's performance on a particular task. Scales often are three-point: skill, emerging; skill, developing; exemplary. Sometimes the qualitative differences in performance are more effectively leveled in five points: emerging, developing, nearly proficient, proficient, exemplary.

*Checklists* offer a way to keep track of learning skills by pre-determining or listing the skills for a period of time or subject of study.

*Questionnaires* are often used as a preassessment activity to show what learners already know about a topic.

*Criterion-referenced assessment* refers to comparing the learner against a predetermined list of skills, concepts, or practices. Often, these criteria are drawn from state or local standards, subject-matter guides, texts, or commercially prepared assessment instruments. All learners are expected to meet the established criteria to demonstrate learning of the subject or skill. This assessment method often is combined with an approach to teaching called *mastery learning*, an approach to teaching and learning that requires reteaching of concepts and skills until all learners can perform at the expected level.

Besides all of the classroom-based assessment techniques that you will choose as you plan learning activities, you will need to be a good consumer of *standardized* assessment measures designed to compare the performance of children on a topic, concept, or skill. Teachers see these measures most frequently as the achievement tests used to measure learning progress at third grade. Other standardized measures commonly used by school psychologists, speech therapists, and specialists in learning disabilities include intelligence tests, language and speech measures, and individualized achievement tests.

In preschool settings, commonly used standardized measures are *screening instruments*, assessment activities, or structured observations that show a brief look at each learner on learning domain or curricular activities. Young children, screened at the beginning of the school year or at a time when progress questions emerge, are quickly reviewed. Most children pass through the screen and only a few may be referred for a more in-depth examination of learning progress. Since these instruments focus "on the big picture" of the developing child or emerging curricular understandings, the results will only link holistically to instructional planning. Any screening measures that identify progress with social–emotional development may be useful for thinking about classroom organization or individualized modifications to support learners with special needs. While screening procedures are most often associated with preschool assessment, instruments can be used at any grade level to gather high point or brief views of child strengths, developmentally or instructionally. However, when teaching in the primary grades, you will most often encounter standardized achievement tests, particularly in third grade. Federal legislation (PL No Child Left Behind, 2001) requires nationwide assessment of progress in reading and mathematics. States may elect to assess achievement in other subject areas. States develop or choose achievement tests to gather this data.

## Standardized Measures in the Process

Standardized measures are *norm-referenced*, in that they compare children's performances. Usually the comparison is based on a national sample of children so that an individual child's performance can be described as typical or atypical for three-year-olds. At third grade, children are compared for reading, mathematics, social studies, or other standards and judged to be *at*, *below*, or *above* the expected performance for third-graders. These standardized measures are best used for program evaluation and curriculum modification based on results for whole-class profiles. For example, if the third-graders do not perform well on items relating to reading and interpreting maps and charts, the teachers might review the curricular emphasis placed on these skills and either increase attention to the skills or choose alternate ways to involve children in learning these skills.

## Reporting to Stakeholders

Once teachers gather the evidence about the progress of learning, various others in the educational arena expect reports of learning. To a certain extent, the nature of the expected report varies by the age of the child, the program philosophy, and any legal requirements for reporting. As you plan the year of assessment activities for your curriculum, you will want to include several of the following reporting methods.

*Informal conferences with students* occur as a usual and customary part of the school day. At the conclusion of a theme or project, such conferences offer teacher and student an opportunity to agree upon accomplishments and next steps.

*Parent conferences* are typically scheduled at the beginning of an enrollment period and at regular intervals—quarterly or midyear and end-of-year. At these times, parents have an opportunity to raise learning concerns, share developmental progress or concerns, and learn how the family might contribute to the development of their child. Portfolios are often an important artifact used in this process.

*Report cards* can become an important part of a child's permanent educational history. Sometimes these reports are narrative in nature. Narratives are written by teachers to show progress in predetermined developmental or subject areas. Increasingly, narrative reports are eliminated in favor of more "objective" reports that show individual child progress compared to criteria or standards. At the preschool level, these may be developmental checklists showing the skills of children on cognitive, physical, and social–emotional scales. In addition, there may be a place for teachers to write brief comments about the child's progress. At the primary level, the checklists usually focus on academic subjects, where progress is noted according to criteria or by assigned grades.

*Grades* are an arbitrary letter or number that represents a summary judgment of child learning. They give little specific information about learning status. In some primary grades, you may be required to use grades. If so, you should plan to supplement this judgment with illustrations of each child's understandings and skills.

## Summary

This chapter described the assessment cycle that applies to curriculum and instruction. Thus, starting with the "What shall be taught?" to "How shall the accomplishment of learning be measured or documented?" the processes and issues related to assessment in social studies and social learning were delineated. In addition, there was a focus on specific techniques for assessment. Parental involvement as part of the assessment plan was highlighted. Reporting to parents, as well as other stakeholders, was described as part of a holistic assessment process. Finally, a link was drawn between classroom assessment and standardized assessment.

## Activities in the Field

1. Visit historical sites and museums in your community. Learn about the resources that they have for teachers. Share with your colleagues.

2. Collect maps of your state and local communities. Compare these to maps found for the historical periods that you plan to teach.

3. If possible, watch children as they are assessed for Child Find or Screening and at high-stakes assessment times. Compare these experiences to daily life in the classroom assessment activities.

## Activities in the Library

1. Go the What Works Clearinghouse: http://www.whatworks.ed. gov/. Examine the standards across the nation. Think about how you might implement these standards while preserving a constructivist approach to learning.

2. Using a search engine such as Google, type in a topic that you are responsible for teaching. Identify authentic assessment methods embedded in the lesson plans, resource sites that you discover.

## Study Questions

1. How should teachers plan lessons that incorporate standards, a constructivist approach to teaching, and embed assessment?

2. How can you incorporate holistic assessment activities into teaching?

3. How should rubrics be developed? How can you involve children?

4. What are some ways to incorporate authentic assessment in lessons?

5. What are appropriate artifacts to include in portfolios to document child learning?

6. How can parents contribute to the assessment process?

7. How do you match the assessment method to the lesson and record-keeping tasks?

8. Where do standardized tests fit in the early childhood picture?

9. What is the responsibility of teachers in using assessment as part of reporting to stakeholders?

## Reflect and Re-read

1. How does assessment of children support the development of curriculum?

2. How do children evolve in their abilities to evaluate their own performance?

## Suggested Further Readings

Chapman, C. (2004). *Differentiated assessment strategies: One tool doesn't fit everyone.* Thousand Oaks, CA: Corwin.

Gullo, D. F. (2005). *Understanding assessment and evaluation in early childhood education* (2nd ed.). New York: Teachers College.

Helms, J. H., Beneke, S., & Steinheimer, K. (1998). *Windows on learning: Documenting young children's work.* New York: Teachers College.

Jablon, J. R., Dombro, A. L., & Dichtelmiller, M. L. (1999). *The power of observation.* Washington, DC: Teaching Strategies. This very readable book is chock full of examples and suggested procedures for making observation efficient and effective.

Johnson, D. W., & Johnson, R. T. (2003). *Assessing students in groups.* Thousand Oaks, CA: Corwin. Practical ways to assess the effectiveness of collaboration.

Mindes, G. (2007). *Assessing young children* (3rd ed.). Englewood Cliffs, NJ: Prentice-Hall/Merrill. Addresses theory and provides illustrations of appropriate practice for prospective teachers, It approaches assessment as an integral part of the teaching-learning process.

## References

Gestwicki, C. (2004). *Home, school, and community relations* (5th ed.). Clifton Park, NY: Thomson/Delmar.

Jacobs, H. H. (Ed.). (2004). *Getting results with curriculum mapping* (pp. 15–16). Alexandria, VA: Association for Supervision and Curriculum Development.

Knoff, H. M. (2001). *The stop and think social skills program: Teacher's manual for PreK-1.* Longmont, CO: Sopris West.

Venn, E. C., & Jahn, M. D. (2004). *Teaching and learning in preschool: Using individually appropriate practices in early childhood literacy instruction.* Newark, DE: International Reading Association.

Wiggins, G. P., & McTighe, J. (2001). *Understanding by design.* Upper Saddle River, NJ: Merrill/ASCD.

### Web Sites

Buros Institute of Mental Measurements http://www.unl.edu/buros. This site publishes reviews of commercially published tests.

National Center for Research on Evaluation Standards and Student Testing http://cresst96.cse.ucla.edu. A website devoted to dissemination of research and illustrations of "best practice" in schools.

## CHAPTER 8

# Knitting It All Together

As Mankind becomes more liberal, they will be more apt to allow that all those who conduct themselves as worthy members of the community are equally entitled to the protections of civil government. I hope ever to see America among the foremost nations of justice and liberality. George Washington (1789)

## Terms to Know

- Big ideas
- Higher-order thinking
- Scope and sequence
- Project-based learning
- Thematic strands of the social studies
- Graphic organizer
- Common good

## Overview

This chapter places social studies at the center of curricular planning. Since social studies is both content and process, there is an opportunity to implement the "big ideas" of social studies using the problem-solving strategies and investigation techniques from the social sciences to foster critical thinking. Big ideas are the enduring or significant questions that when implemented foster *higher-order thinking*—thinking that demands connection of concepts, skills, and dispositions. Excerpts of content learning standards for mathematics, science, and language arts illustrate the broad connectors for integrated learning projects. This chapter includes examples of thematic instructional units for preschool and primary experiences.

## Focus Questions

1. What is the history of social studies education as a curriculum integrator?
2. How do you use inquiry-based questions effectively in preschool?
3. How do you use the developmental scope and sequence of social studies in concert with the child-inquiry questions to develop units?

## Applying the Traditions of Social Studies

The social studies tradition of holistic instruction (cf. Maxim, 2006) continues to the present day with the *scope*—usual grade level—and *sequence*—the order and extent of content—for the social studies in elementary school defined as follows:

- Kindergarten—awareness of self in social setting
- First grade—the individual in school and family life
- Second grade—the neighborhood.
- Third grade—sharing the earth with others in the community. (National Council for Social Studies [NCSS], 1984, pp. 376–385)

Textbooks and state standards for the primary grades focus on this developmental sequence of topics and interests as well as other broad themes. Preschool programs often explore these topics as well. At each level of exploration, the depth and breadth of topic can expand.

## The Preschool Years

Therefore, prior to elementary school, in the preschool years, the content focus of social studies relies on the concepts of self-understanding with activities to support the development of self-control, feelings of confidence, and an awareness of growing physical and intellectual competence. Common activities include reading and discussing books about self. Example activities are shown below.

## "Who am I?" activities

Answering the phone at home:

- Who answers?
- What is the greeting?
- What information can you give to unknown persons?
- What do you say to the caller when parents, caregiver, or sibling are busy?

Discuss some scenarios for survey researcher, telemarketer, charity solicitation, PTA president, or other unknown adult. Ask children to share their experiences with phone answering. Ask them to identify good strategies for phone answering. This activity promotes *responsibility* and an assessment of self-responsibility and the limits of responsibility, e.g. hanging up the phone is always an option.

Expand the discussion to other situations where children must exercise judgment and demonstrate self-confidence.

Suggested books to extend the activity: Bemelmans, L. (2000) *Madeline's rescue*. East Rutherford, NJ: Viking Jr. and Loomis, C., & Poydar, N. (1994) *At the mall*. New York: Scholastic. (*Source*: Adapted from Mindes and Donovan, 2001).

Choosing and using personal character trait vocabulary for self-exploration:

Read *Brown Bear, Brown Bear* (Martin, B. (1994) Twinsburg, OH: K&M International) to the class, emphasizing the repeated phrase, "I see a...looking at me." Ask children to think about traits that describe them. Then hold a mirror before each child and repeat the phrase. "Mirror, mirror what do you see?" Child says, I see a caring, kind, responsible boy/girl looking at me. This activity can be done individually or in small groups. Other identity characteristics can be included: I see a strong, athletic, demure, leader, etc. looking at me.

Follow-up activities include self-portraits, charts to describe the characteristics of the class, and graphs that summarize the numbers of children possessing particular traits.

Suggested books to extend the activity: Albrough, J. (1990) *Beaky*. Boston: Houghton Mifflin and Carle, E. (1998) *The mixed-up chameleon*. Scrantdon, PA: HarperCollins. (*Source*: Adapted from Mindes and Donovan, 2001).

Following is a list of suggested books to use to advance this learning and develop self-concept, self-efficacy.

Alexander, M. (1973). *When the new baby comes, I'm moving out.* East Rutherford, NJ: Dial.

Bailey, B., & Burdock, L. A. (2004). *Shubert's big voice.* Oviedo, FL: Loving Guidance.

Boynton, S. (1983). *A is for angry.* New York: Workman.

Brighton, C. (1984). *My hand, my world.* New York: Macmillan.

Bunting, E., & Meddaugh, S. (1996). *No nap.* Boston: Houghton Mifflin.

Carle, E. (1986). *The grouchy ladybug.* New York: HarperCollins.

Carlson, N. (1988). *I like me.* East Rutherford, NJ: Puffin.

Cooney, N. (1981). *The blanket that had to go.* East Rutherford, NJ: Putnam.

Cosby, B. (1997). *The meanest thing to say.* New York: Scholastic;

Emberly, E., & Miranda, A. (1997). *Glad monster, sad monster: A book about feelings.* New York: Little Brown.

Henkes, K. (1986). *A weekend with Wendell.* Scranton, PA: Morrow.

Hoban, L. (1985). *Arthur's loose tooth.* Scranton, PA: Harper & Row.

Hutchins, P. (1983). *You'll soon grow into them, Titch.* Fairfield, NJ: Greenwillow.

Jonas, A. (1991). *When you were a baby.* Fairfield, NJ: Greenwillow.

Lionni, L. (1960). *Inch by inch.* New York: HarperCollins.

Miller, K. (2000). *Did my first mother love me?* Chicago: Independent Publishers Group.

Norac, C. (2004). *My daddy is a giant.* East Rutherford, NJ: Clarion.

Parker, S. (1994). *How the body works.* Toronoto, Canada: Dorling Kindersley Limited.

Rukhsans, K. (2005). *Silly chicken.* London:Viking.

Thomas, J. R. (1991). *The wish card ran out!* New York: HarperCollins.

van Dordt, E., & Westerink, G. (1998). *Am I really that different?* Edinburgh, UK: Floris.

Wiseman, B. (1991). *Morris goes to school.* New York: HarperCollins.

Wojciechowski, S. (2005). *Beany and the Meany.* Cambridge, MA: Candlewick.

Zolotow, C. (1963). *The quarrelling book.* Scranton, PA: Harper & Row.

In addition, the preschool social studies curricular content explores group living and develops understandings of self in family and "school" environments. Examples of classroom community activities are presented here, along with selected children's literature selections to support these themes.

## Best friends at school

At the beginning of the school year, start a discussion with young children to think about how friends care for each other, e.g. help button coat, smile across the room, and wait to speak while someone else is talking. Then, think about rude behavior. What does it look like? Why does it hurt? Why can't we be rude in class?

Extend this activity by planning a skit that shows the class that cares for the community of learners.

Suggested books to extend the activity: Baer, E. (1992) *This is the way we go to school.* New York: Scholastic; Bunnett, R. (1995) *Friends at school.* Long Island City, NY: Star Bright; and Testa, M. (1994) *Thumbs up, Rico!* Morton Grove, IL: Albert Whitman. (Source: Adapted from Mindes and Donovan, 2001, pp. 126–127).

## Who Can Help?

Gather students on the rug. Show the class the Yellow Pages. If you want help with a pet, who do you see? If we need help with a leaky faucet, who do you call? How do you know where to look for this information?

Now, let's think about who can help at school. If we have questions about lunch menus, who do we call? If we want to know when spring vacation begins, who do we ask? If we want to read a book on trucks, who can help?

Then, help the children make a School Yellow Pages with pictures taken by the children and labels prepared by teachers. Give each child a Yellow Page that they can use to hold pictures taken by friends or teachers that shows how they can help in the class community.

Suggested books to extend this activity: Anholt, C., & Anholt, L. (1992) *All about you.* Anchorage, AK: Viking; Kasza, K. (2000) *Don't laugh, Joe.* East Rutherford, NJ: Putnam Juvenile; and Rathmann, P. (1993) *Ruby the copy-cat.* New York: Scholastic. (Source: Adapted from Mindes and Donovan, 2001, pp. 132–133)

## Typical Preschool Social Studies Themes

Who am I?
Who is my family?
How does my family play?
What work does my family do?
How does my family celebrate?
What are my family traditions?

What pets live in my house?
Where do I live?
What kinds of houses are in my neighborhood?
How do we get around?
How do we make a class community?
Where does our food come from?

The content is drawn from child curiosities and implemented with strategies that foster inquiry-based and *project-based learning*—teachers and children investigate topics from multiple perspectives (cf. Katz & Chard, 2001). In this approach, teachers construct activities with children that enhance development of self-understanding by engaging children in hands-on, child-chosen topics. The strategies employed foster investigatory skills when the questions are derived from child curiosity. Finally the approach promotes cooperative learning and enhanced appreciation of cultural diversity in the community of the classroom with activities structured to scaffold children's budding group work skills.

Some examples of significant questions that preschoolers can investigate are presented here.

## Books on Families and School

*Families*

Alexander, M. (1971). *Nobody asked me if I wanted a baby sister.* East Rutherford, NJ: Dial.
Asch, F. (1981). *My mother travels a lot.* London: Warner.
Baker, S. A. (1995). *Grandpa is a flyer.* Morton Grove, IL: Albert Whitman.
Blumenthal, D. (1999). *The chocolate-covered cookie tantrum.* Boston: Clarion.
Beskow, A. (2001). *Aunt green, aunt brown & aunt lavender.* Edinburgh, UK: Floris.
Butterworth, N. (1989). *My mom is fantastic.* Livermore, CA: Discovery Toys.
Crewes, N. (1998). *You are here.* New York: Greenwillow Books.
Dooley, N. (1995). *Everybody bakes bread.* Minneapolis: Carolrhoda Books.
Dooley, N. (1992). *Everybody cooks rice.* Minneapolis: First Avenue Editions.
Drescher, J. (1986). *My mother's getting married.* East Rutherford, NJ: Dial.
Greene, S. (1998). *Show and tell.* Boston: Clarion.
Hines, A. G. (1999). *Daddy makes the best spaghetti.* Boston: Clarion.
Hoopes. L. L. (1984). *My daddy's coming home.* Scranton, PA: Harper & Row.
Levine, E. (1995). *I hate English.* New York: Scholastic.

Lindsay, J. (2000). *Do I have a daddy?* Chicago: Independent Publishers Group.

Oxenberry, H. (1984). *Grandpa and grandma.* East Rutherford, NJ: Dial.

Pitts, M. (1983). *My mommy needs me.* Fairfield, NJ: Lothrop, Lee & Shepard.

Sanchez, J. (1988). *The giant child.* Doral, FL: Santillana USA.

Scarry, R. (1968). *What do people do all day?* New York: Random House.

Sendak, M. (1992). *Chicken soup with rice.* New York: Scholastic.

Seward, W. (2001). *Good night daddy.* Chicago: Independent Publishers Group.

Sharmot, M. W. (1993). *A big fat enormous lie.* New York: Penquin-Putnam.

Stein, S. B. (1979). *The adopted one.* New York: Walker.

Steptoe, J. (1987). *Mufaro's beautiful daughters.* Scranton, PA: Lothrop, Lee & Shepard.

Vigna, J. (1981). *Daddy's new baby.* Morton Grove, IL: Albert Whitman.

Vigna, J. (1987). *Mommy and me by ourselves again.* Morton Grove, IL: Whitman.

Weininger, B. (2000). *Will you mind the baby Davy.* New York: Michael Neugebauer.

Wilhoite, M. (1991). *Daddy's roommate.* Los Angeles: Alyson Books.

Ziefert, H. (1993). *Harry takes a bath.* New York: Puffin.

Zemach, M. (1990). *It could always be worse.* New York: Farrar, Straus, & Giroux.

## School

Austin, V. (1996). *Say please.* Cambridge, MA: Candlewick.

Baer, E. (1992). *This is the way we go to school.* Scranton, PA: Scholastic.

Brown, T. (1995). *Someone's special just like you.* New York: Henry Holt.

Bunnett, R. (1996). *Friends at school.* Long Island City, NY: Star Bright Books.

Cazet, D. (1990). *Never spit on your shoes.* Scranton, PA: Orchard.

Cazet, D. (1993). *Born in the gravy.* Scranton, PA: Orchard.

Cohen, M. (1967). *Will I have a friend?* New York: Macmillan.

Cosby, B. (1999). *Hooray for the warrior dandelions!* New York: Scholastic.

Giff, P. R. (1988). *All about Stacy.* New York: Random House.

Giff, P. R. (1988). *B-E-S-T friends.* New York: Random House.

Gomi, T. (1995). *My friends.* San Francisco: Chronicle Books.

Henkes, K. (1996). *Chrysanthemum.* New Hyde Park, NY: Mulberry.

Hoffman, M. (1991). *Amazing grace.* East Rutherford, NJ: Dial.

Jackson, E. (2003). *It's back to school we go! First day stories from around the world.* Brockfield, CT: Millbrook.

**Table 8.1**
**Child Queries and Related Social Studies Themes**

| Child Query | Social Studies Theme |
| --- | --- |
| Where do groceries come from? | Production, distribution, and consumption |
| How do people travel to work? | Science, technology, and society |
| What kind of structures do we live in? | People, places, and environments |
| Who lives in my house? | Culture; Individual development and identity |
| How do we care for pets? | People, places, and environments |
| What is justice in the classroom? | Power, authority, and governance |
| What kind of TV did grandma/grandpa watch? | Science, technology, and society |

Jahn-Clough, L. (1999). *My friend and I.* Boston: Houghton Mifflin.

Kraus, R. (1994). *Leo the late bloomer.* Scranton, PA: Harper Trophy.

Laskey, K. (1996). *Lunch bunnies.* New York: Little Brown.

Lillegard, D. (2003). *Hello school!* New York: Random House.

McCully, E. A. (2005). *School.* Scranton, PA: HarperCollins.

Powell, J. (1999). *Talking about disability.* Chicago: Raintree.

Senisi, E. B. (1994). *Kindergarten kids.* Minneapolis: Cartwheel Books.

Wilde, O. (1995). *The selfish giant.* East Rutherford, NJ: Putnam.

Wiseman, B. (1991). *Morris goes to school.* Scranton, PA: HarperCollins.

These questions are associated with the *thematic strands within social studies* or organizing categories derived from the social sciences as developed by the NCSS (Table 8.1). Ten broad themes of the social studies are culture; time continuity and change; people, places, and environments; individual development and identity; individuals, groups, and institutions; power, authority, and governance; production, distribution, and consumption; science, technology, and society; global connections; and civic ideals and practices (NCSS, 1994).

In studying the content of these themes, the implementation of the processes of social studies consists of the disciplines of anthropology, archaeology, economics, geography, history, law, philosophy, political science, psychology, religion, and sociology as their traditional foci (NCSS, 1994).

Thus, using the underlying concepts from social science, teachers draw content broadly from the ten themes and use the inquiry-based processes to foster curiosity, problem-solving skills, and appreciation of investigation to solve classroom questions and school issues as well as investigate neighborhood and community problems with the goal of enhancing understanding along with civic awareness and pride. Therefore, broadly

defined, the social studies in preschool include the disparate, but intertwined, content of the following:

- Social learning in young children, self-concept development, includ-
  ing character development
- Academic content of social studies based on ten themes (NCSS, 1994)
- Classroom community development
- Foundational understandings for civic engagement

Both as content and process, the social studies focus on a whole-
child orientation. The social studies build from social interactions and
child-constructed meaning. These studies help children acquire the required academic material proposed by state and national standards. Finally, by beginning with the knowledge, skills, and dispositions of the
children in particular classes, teachers reinforce an inextricable link among
family, culture, and community while facilitating the learning of social
studies. As young children explore themes, teachers make transparent the
understandings about all of the different kinds of families, their cultures,
and the community context. That is, teachers consciously link the understandings gleaned from one theme to the next. Families have cultural beliefs, customs, and artifacts; the community is made up of people and families from diverse backgrounds.

In the section that follows, see an example of how to use a social studies
tool to explore child questions, linking to reading. The assumption behind
the material that follows is that the teacher and children are interested in
developing understandings about maps that they will use throughout the
year. Presumably, such investigation folds into other investigations that
the class made about self, family, and school. In the following section, an
example is shown that illustrates how a teacher tries to be responsive to
child interests as well as responsive to the demands for compliance with
state standards. Thus, the teacher thinks about child interest in maps and
state standards and begins a thematic unit of study by reading a book
about maps.

## Thematic Unit: Maps[1]

Ms. Dritz and her students were interested in beginning to learn about
maps. The class read together *My Map Book* (Fanelli, 1995) as a starting
point. Ms. Dritz wanted to select and create activities that would build on
a student's desire to accumulate knowledge of maps and the geographical
ideas that can be included in such a unit. Objectives are selected from
standards set by the Illinois State Board of Education. IL Goal 17 of social

science states that children should, "Understand world geography and the effects of geography on society." To reach this goal Ms. Dritz chooses an activity that introduces students to geography.

The benchmarks include both "locating objects and places in familiar environments" and "expressing beginning geographic thinking." Ms. Dritz wanted a well-rounded unit, so she reviewed the objectives for all developmental domains. For physical development and health, she referred to IL Goal 16, wherein the benchmarks include "engaging in active play using gross motor skills" and "engaging in activity play using fine motor skills." She also addresses the domain of fine arts by incorporating IL Goal 26. This goal states that, "through creating and performing, understand how works of art are produced." She includes activities that meet the benchmarks of "participating in dance, drama, music, and visual arts." Through other activities, she will incorporate IL Goal 25's benchmark of the student's ability to "describe or respond to their own creative work or the creative work of others."

Objectives for social–emotional development will be to meet IL Goal 31, "developing an awareness of personal identity and positive self concept." Objectives for the Language Arts domain will address the benchmarks under IL Goal 1 that will give the children an "understanding that pictures and symbols have meaning and that print carries a message." By planning activities that compare distance and location through maps, the class will be addressing the Mathematics developmental domain. Under IL Goal 7, the activities offer opportunities to achieve "a beginning understanding of measurement using non-standard units and measurement words." The science domain IL Goal 12 facilitates children's progress toward the goal of "understanding the fundamental concepts, principles, and interconnections of the life, physical and earth/space sciences." Thus, Ms. Dritz has incorporated child interest and planned activities to support state goals.

## Activity

Materials: the book *My Map Book* (Fanelli, S. (1995), New York: HarperCollins)
Learning Center: Book and Library Center
Domains Covered:

Social–emotional

Social science

Language Arts

Science

**Table 8.2**
**Maps**

| Know | Want to know | Learned |
|---|---|---|
| Maps are pictures of places. | How to draw maps? | Will be completed at the end of the investigation |
| Maps show locations of things in a place. | Where to find ready-made maps? | |
| Maps show you how to go places. | How people use maps? | |

To introduce the unit she uses *My Map Book* (Fanelli, 1995). Ms. Dritz chose to begin the theme with this book because she believes it is important to start at a "self" level with the child to capture child interest in the topic at hand. *My Map Book* supports this strategy by starting with what the child already knows and can relate to their personal lives. The book contains a series of maps that look like child drawings. This makes the book uniquely appealing to the children. It offers a map of a heart, for example, which will help place feeling into a map and trigger development of self in the social–emotional domain. It also includes a map of a tummy, which can cover a science objective, because it gives a child a look into how food travels to the stomach. So, after reading the book, Ms. Dritz will assist children in identifying the following: What do you know about maps? What do you want to learn? At the conclusion of the investigation, the children will document what they have learned. This graphic organizer—Know, Want to Know, Learned (KWL)—assists both teacher and children as the investigation advances.

In the next planning example, Ms. Hudzik outlines a thematic unit on community helpers. This topic is required by the child care agency where she teaches. Look at the planning grid to see how the principles of constructivist are incorporated even though the topic emerges from the teacher.

## Thematic Unit: Community Helpers[2]

**Weekly Lesson Plan**
**Week of**: February 7, 2005
**Teacher:** Maggie Hudzik
**Study/Project:** Community/Community Helpers
**Assistant:** Ima Helper

## Weekly Lesson Plan

| Learning Centers | Monday | Tuesday | Wednesday | Thursday | Friday |
|---|---|---|---|---|---|
| Blocks | Regular blocks | Blocks with cars added | Blocks with cars added | Blocks with cars and stop sign added | Blocks with stop sign added |
| Art | Make signs for the community | Have the students paint themselves as a community helper | Regular Art Corner set up | Regular Art Corner set up | Construct school bus, signs, and other community artifacts |
| Sand and Water | Normal sand and water | Add cars to sand and water | Add cars and construction vehicles to sand and water | Add cars and construction vehicles to sand and water | Add cars and construction vehicles to sand and water |
| Computers | During free time: Latches Fire Truck computer game | During free time: Latches Fire Truck computer game | During free time: Latches Fire Truck computer game | During free time: Latches Fire Truck computer game | During free time: Latches Fire Truck computer game |
| Outdoors | Take a walk around the community (about 15 minutes) | No outdoor time | No outdoor time | Have tour of a fire truck from the fire department | No outdoor time |
| Music and Movement | Walking through the neighborhood | Sing and dance to "When I Grow Up" | "Stretch for the Doctor" | Dance and sing "The Little Red Fire Truck" | Sing "The Wheels on the Bus" |
| Library | Read "I Love Signs" plus extra community books in library | Read "Community Helpers from A–Z" plus extra community books in library | Read "I Want to be a Doctor" plus extra community books in library | Read "The Little Fireman" plus extra community books in library | Read "School Bus" plus extra community books in library |
| Dramatic Play | Regular kitchen area | Doctor's Office dramatic play | Doctor's Office dramatic play | Doctor's Office dramatic play and mail area setup | Doctor's Office dramatic play and mail area setup |
| Toys and Games | Regular toys and games | Add doctor things (stethoscope, doctor's coat, thermometer, etc.) Set up a little office in kitchen area | Add doctor things (stethoscope, doctor's coat, thermometer, etc.) Set up a little office in kitchen area | Play the "Ladder Game." Add letters, mailbag, and mailbox | Add letters, mailbag, and mailbox |
| Discovery | Walking through the neighborhood | Voting: What community helper do we want to be? | Regular discovery toys and activities | Regular discovery toys and activities | Voting: How do we get to school? |
| Cooking | No cooking | Faces of the community: Using bread, fruits and nuts, etc. | No cooking | No cooking | No cooking |

## Objectives and Goals

### Objective

To learn who is very important in our community, such as firemen and doctors, or even a mayor. The children would learn what their responsibility is for the community.

### Learning Goal

IL 14: D: EC—Develop an awareness of goals of leaders in their environment.

### Objective

Have the students become familiar with voting.

### Learning Goal

IL 14: C: EC—Participate in voting as a way of making choices.

## Skills and Concepts the Children Will Develop

Hopefully, the students will grasp a serious concept on what a community is and what it entails. Also, the students should be able to have an understanding of what kind of people make up the community and how they help. The students should have some understanding of how a community works and how it is run, such as with voting.

## Materials Needed

*Community Helpers from A to Z* (Kalman, B. 1998 New York: Crabtree), *The Little Fireman* (Brown, M. W. 1993, New York: HarperCollins), *I Want to Be a Doctor* (Liebman, D. 2002, Toronto: Firefly), *School Bus* (Crews, D. 1983 New York: HarperCollins), and active-play toys: doctor's coat, stethoscope, thermometer, etc.; fire department ladder, fireman hat and coat; letters and envelopes, mailbag, and mailbox. Bread, fruits (dried and fresh), spoons, poster boards and stickers, extra books for library revolving around the community, Latches Fire Truck computer game, toy cars and stop signs, toy construction vehicles, popsicle sticks, triangular pieces of paper, paint and larger pieces of paper, bus cutout sheets, and crayons.

## Evaluation

Observation, such as with the blocks and if they understand stop signs, or with the dramatic play tools, look at their artistic creations, and listen to their comments about the books read and activities done, such as with the fire truck and walk through the community.

The planning examples above represent beginning teacher's explorations using children's curiosity and Illinois learning goals. Note that the teachers are thinking through the process and developing plans that are multidimensional, incorporating various academic content areas. The teachers are thinking through project planning. As the plans are implemented, changes will be made and new plans made in response to child progress. In the next section are examples of the planning process in the primary years.

## The Primary Years

Using the aforementioned scope and sequence of the NCSS (1984), most state curricula and available child texts draw attention to the broad themes of self in kindergarten, family in first grade, neighborhood in second grade, and community in third grade. However, teachers and young children often explore other "big ideas" such as

- How do inventors change lives?
- How do people get money?
- What does the rainforest contribute to global environment?
- How do immigrants come to Nebraska?
- Who makes the clothes we wear?
- Where does the trash go?

Through the exploration of these "big ideas," the social studies offer a structure for broad theme-based content. Content organized around a topic offers multiple entry points and significant opportunities for investigation, and represents a training ground for students to acquire problem-solving skills, as well as providing a laboratory for the development and elaboration of interpersonal coping skills and strategies. "The primary purpose of social studies is to help young people develop the ability to make informed and reasoned decisions for the public good as citizens of a culturally diverse, democratic society in an interdependent world" (NCSS, 1994, 3). Accordingly, children develop a sense of civic responsibility through the exploration of rich, thematic studies. As well, children use and elaborate other information-gathering and concept-formation aptitudes by applying subject-matter knowledge, skills, and dispositions from other subject-matter concentrations—reading, mathematics, science, and the arts.

Using these themes as starting points, children and teachers form hypotheses, gather data, summarize, and make conclusions. Finally, children organize and present the data. Not only are children using the skills of the social scientists in these investigations, and learning about civic engagement, but they are also reading, managing, and displaying data. The strategies for instruction in the social studies include individual investigations in the library, in the field, on the Internet, interviewing, small-group collaboration, and large-group discussions. Examples of these techniques are shown in the sample thematic units as well as throughout this text.

Through use of social studies themes, teachers integrate the seemingly distinct goals into meaningful investigations. Using a developmentally appropriate practice model (Bredekamp & Copple, 1997), teachers can develop the natural social studies curriculum. Caveats for thematic curriculum include attention to the following:

- Build on what children already know
- Develop concepts and processes of social studies rather than focus on isolated facts
- Provide hands-on activities
- Use the content and processes relevantly throughout the year
- Capitalize on child interest. (Katz & Chard, 2001)

Developed in this way, the curricula of social studies use big ideas to connect with children and facilitate their increased understanding of their relevant social world.

With the current public focus on patriotism and the symbolism of nationalism and democracy, children in a first grade became curious about symbols of democracy in the United States. In the next section is an example of a two-week study created to begin the exploration.

## Examples of Good Practice in Action

This illustration shows how a first-grade unit begins from the required curricular directive to incorporate the study of the symbols of the United

States. Note the children's literature and Web sites collected to begin this investigation

**Theme:** What Does America Stand For?[3]

**Grade Level:** First

**Context of the Unit:**

- Unit would best fit in the spring season
  - Leads into Memorial Day/Summer/July 4th season
  - Community would be the focus of the fall season
  - Holidays around the world would be the focus of the winter season

**NCSS Curriculum Strand(s) Addressed:**

- Culture
- Time, continuity, and change
- People, places, and environments
- Individual development and identity
- Individuals, groups, and institutions
- Power, authority, and governance
- Civic ideals and practices

**Core Thematic Questions Explored:**

- What is a symbol?
- What symbols represent America?
- What do the following mean in America?
  - Democracy
  - American flag
  - Statue of Liberty
  - The White House
  - George Washington
  - George Bush
  - The Great Seal
  - National Holidays

## *Key Vocabulary*

| | | |
|---|---|---|
| State | Nation | America |
| Vote | Holiday | Freedom |
| Symbol | Friend | Flag |
| Statue | Fatder | Quarter |
| Penny | Dime | Dollar |
| Country | Honesty | White House |
| President | U.S.A. | |

*Source:* Created by Elizabeth Borg and Mollie Sutfin, DePaul University, teacher candidates.

## *Summary of Resources for Children, Teachers, and Families Literature*

### Books Used for Instruction

*Flags of the World* (2003) by W.D. Crampton and William Crampton. Tulsa, OK: Usborne Books.

*Pinky Promise: A Book About Telling the Truth* (2004) by Vanita Braver. Washington, DC: Child & Family Press.

*Red, White and Blue: The Story of the American Flag* (1998) by John Herman. East Rutherford, NJ: Putnam.

*So You Want To Be President* (2000) by Judith St. George. New York: Penguin.

*The Statue of Liberty* (2001) by Lloyd G. Douglas. New York: Scholastic.

*The Story of the White House* (1992) by Kate Waters. New York: Scholastic.

*Young George Washington: America's First President* (1997) by Andrew Woods. Mahwah, NJ: Troll Books.

### Books Used for Independent Investigation

*A Flag for All* (2003) by Larry Dane Brimner and Christine Trip. Danbury, CT: Children's Press.

*Benny's Flag* (2003) by Phyllis Krasilovsky. Lanham, MD: Roberts Rinehart Publishers.

*Betsy Ross* (1998) by Alexandra Wallner. New York: Holiday House.

*George Washington's Breakfast.* (1998) by Jean Fritz. New York: Putnam.

*George Washington's Socks* (1993) by Elvira Woodruff. New York: Scholastic.

*George Washington's Teeth* (2003) by Deborah Chandra and Madeleine Comora. Gordonsville, VA: Farrar, Strauss & Giroux.

*. . . If You Grew Up with George Washington* (1993) by Ruth Belov Gross. New York: Scholastic.

*I Know About Flags* (1995) by Chris Jaeggi and Meyer Seltzer Chicago: Rand McNally.

*I Wonder Why Countries Fly Flags and Other Questions about People and Places* (1995) by Claude Steele. Helena, MT: Kingfisher.

*Magic Treehouse #22: Revolutionary War on Wednesday* (2000) by Mary Pope Osbourne. New York: Random House.

*Meet George Washington* (2001) by Joan Heilbroner. New York: Random House.

*Meet Our Flag, Old Glory* (2004) by April Jones Prince and Joan Paley. Collingdale, PA: DIANE.

*Red, White, and Blue* (2002) by Laurie Knowlton. Dallas: Pelican.

*Take the Lead, George Washington* (2005) by Judith St. George. East Rutherford, NJ:Philomel.

*The Flag Maker* by Susan Campbell Bartoletti and Claire A. Nivola.

*The Pledge of Allegiance* (2000) by F. Bellamy. New York: Scholastic Inc.

*What Freedom Means to Me* (2004) by Heather French Henry. Woodland Hills, CA: Cubbie Blue.

### Technology/Web Sites

### For Teachers

*History: Statue of Liberty.* American Park Network. Retrieved May 1, 2005, at 4:06 PM from http://www.americanparknetwork.com/parkinfo/sl/history/liberty.html.

*History of the Flag of the United States of America.* Retrieved April 25, 2005, at 10:15 AM from http://www.usflag.org/history.html.

*The Story of the Pledge of Allegiance.* Retrieved April 25, 2005, at 10:12 AM from http://www.flagday.org/Pages/StoryofPledge.html.

### For Students

*Count Change.* Retrieved May 11, 2005, at 2:30 PM from www.internet 4classrooms.com.

*If I Were President...* Scholastic. Retrieved April 26, 2005, at 5:05 PM from http://teacher.scholastic.com/products/instructor/president. htm.

*The Democracy Project: President for the Day.* PBS Kids Go! Retrieved May 3, 2005, at 1:14 PM from http://pbskids.org/democracy/presforaday/index.html.

## *Social Studies Activities—Monday to Friday*

What is a symbol?
National Holidays
We the People
Red, White, and Blue (American Flag)
Standing for Friendship and Freedom (Statue of Liberty)
A Day in the Life of the White House
Father of Our Country
The Day I Became President
The Great Seal
National Holiday Book

In the following section are examples of two social studies lessons derived from this unit.

**Thursday—Focus Day**

**8:30–8:45 Calendar**

**8:45–8:50 Pledge of Allegiance**

**8:50–9:50 Social Studies**

Grade Level: 1st
Number of Students: 20
Approximate Length: 60 minutes
Social Studies Area Focus: What Does America Stand For?
Activity #4 Name: Red, White, and Blue

Materials:

- American flag
- *Red, White and Blue: The Story of the American Flag*
- Journal worksheet page for booklet
- Red, white, and blue star stickers
- American flag color page for booklet cover
- Marker and wipe board/chalk and chalkboard

Lesson Objectives:

- Students will learn the history and symbols of the American flag.

- Students will replicate the symbolic parts of the American flag by designing symbols for the twenty-first century that show their concept of America.

Standards
Illinois State Goals:

14.F.1 Describe political ideas and traditions important to the development of the United States including democracy, individual rights, and the concept of freedom.

16.B.1b (US) Explain why individuals, groups, issues and events are celebrated with local, state, or national holidays or days of recognition (e.g., Lincoln's Birthday, Martin Luther King's Birthday, Pulaski Day, Fourth of July, Memorial Day, Labor Day, Veterans' Day, Thanksgiving).

4.B.1b Participate in discussions around a common topic.

3.A.1 Construct complete sentences that demonstrate subject–verb agreement; appropriate capitalization and punctuation; correct spelling of appropriate, high-frequency words; and appropriate use of the eight parts of speech.

Procedure/Method:

1. Begin by having the class recite the "Pledge of Allegiance."
2. Share with the class its history, including who wrote it, why, and how the words have changed over the years.
3. Explain the concept of a symbol (representation) and ask the class to help describe what they think the flag represents (freedom, pride, and unity). This gages the current knowledge of the class on the symbols of the American flag.
4. Tell the class that today we are going to learn about the American flag, what it represents, and its significance in our country.
5. Read to the class *Red, White, and Blue: The Story of the American Flag* by John Herman.
6. Discuss as a class what was surprising in the book and what they thought was the most interesting fact.
7. Give the children 10–15 minutes to write journal entry about what they learned and what the American flag symbolizes (this will be part of an America booklet at the end of the unit).

8. When the students are done writing their journals, ask for some examples of what the students wrote in their journal and write the learnings and symbols on the board.

9. This lesson will culminate as the students work to construct an American flag page that will be used as the cover to their booklets.

10. Students will take what they learned about the stripes, stars, and colors to replicate the flag in their colored pictures.

11. Collect the colored flags and the journal entries.

Assessment/Evaluation:

a. Students will be assessed in their participation and knowledge to share during the discussions on the story and the journal entries.

b. Students will be assessed by the details included in their journal entries. The teacher will not correct or add anything to the entries (as it is free writing) but will add red, white, or blue stars next to key points that students made in their journals.

c. Students will be observed during the making of their booklet cover to see if they can apply what they learned about the physical symbols on the flag to complete their own.

Differentiation:

• The teacher will walk around to aid children in writing, spelling, and thought starters for their journal entries.

• The teacher will aid students in recalling the colors and symbols in coloring their flag.

Enrichment/Extension:
A language arts extension could include a worksheet with the letters F-L-A-G down the left side. Students could work individually or in pairs to come up with a poem beginning with the letters in the word flag. They could be encouraged to include information learned in the lesson of the symbols on the flag.

Closure:

Display flags and twenty-first-century America symbols.

References:

*History of the Flag of the United States of America.* Retrieved April 25, 2005, at 10:15 AM from http://www.usflag.org/history.html.
*The Story of the Pledge of Allegiance.* Retrieved April 25, 2005, at 10:12 AM from http://www.flagday.org/Pages/StoryofPledge.html.

**Tuesday—Focus Day**

**8:30–8:45 Calendar**

**8:45–8:50 Pledge of Allegiance**

**8:50–10:05 Social Studies**

Grade Level: 1st
Number of Students: 20
Approximate Length: 75 minutes
Social Studies Area Focus: What Does America Stand For?
Activity #2 Name: Father of Our Country

Materials:

- Picture(s) of George Washington
- *Young George Washington: America's First President* by Andrew Wood
- Twenty word scramble worksheets (appendix)
- One 1-dollar bill
- Twenty quarters
- Monopoly-sized white paper (students will have pencils or colored pencils/marker/crayons)

Lesson Objectives:

- Students will identify key aspects of George Washington's life and historical contributions.
- Students will demonstrate cooperative learning to determine answers and guide others in completing a word scramble worksheet assignment.

Standards
Illinois State Goals:

14.D.1 Identify the roles of civic leaders (e.g., elected leaders, public service leaders).

4.B.1b Participate in discussions around a common topic.

Procedure/Method:

1. Begin class by asking students to share their definition of a leader
   - Prompt the class with examples of leadership in their own community/environment (principal, mayor, teachers, coach).
   - Write the characteristics that the students share on the board.
   - Ask students why it is important to lead (or have a leader) in certain situations (a leader supports, is an example, makes decisions).

2. Ask the class if anyone knows the name we give to the person who leads our entire country, the United States of America (President).

3. Tell the class that throughout history, there have been 43 presidents of the United States, and today we are going to learn about the very first president, George Washington.

4. Show the class a picture(s) of the first president, pointing out distinct differences in clothes, hair, stance, etc.

5. Read *Young George Washington: America's First President* by Andrew Wood.

6. Lead a discussion about the information in the book, prompting the class with questions particularly related to the word scramble to be completed later in the lesson.

7. Have the students return to their desks and hand out the word scramble worksheet on George Washington (would include words related to Washington's life, scrambled; link to example provided in "references").

8. Explain the process we must go through to allow the letters and the information we learned worked together to come up with the word for the blank.

9. Give students 7–10 minutes to work on the worksheet as individuals, then group them into pods of three to work on the remaining blanks and to share the answers that they have already completed (the groups should be predetermined, matching a range of abilities in each group).

10. Go through the answers as a class, walking through the process for any words that have not been completed.

11. Collect the worksheets and tell the children that they will be a part of their American booklet.

12. Walk around the class with a dollar and a quarter, pointing out that George Washington's face is on both (explain that this is one way that we honor him for all of the things he stood for and accomplished, as we just read about).

13. Give each student a pre-cut piece of white paper (the size of Monopoly money) and a quarter.

14. Demonstrate how you can put the quarter under the paper, take a pencil or colored pencil, and create the imprint on the paper.

15. Allow students the chance to decorate their money any way they would like, with Washington's face in the middle.

16. Hang the new money on a designated board or bulletin area.

Assessment/Evaluation:

- Students will be observed through their participation and answers during the story discussion.
- Students will be observed as they work individually on the word scramble worksheet, and also as they interact in the small group setting to share and determine remaining answers.

Differentiation:

- The teacher will walk around to aid children in the word scramble worksheet.
- Groups will be organized according to different abilities and behavior patterns. The teacher will separate groups who cannot work cooperatively, focused, and as a team.

Enrichment/Extension:

This lesson could extend into the area of language arts as students work to come up with their own word scramble worksheets on any given topic. The teacher can guide the topic to relate to something studied in any subject, such as science, math, or literature. Creating the worksheet will be a review of learned information and facts for each student and will also utilize their writing and spelling skills. The worksheets can be combined as a workbook activity for each student to complete during free time.

Closure:

Discuss places that George Washington is symbolically represented, for example, dollar bill, quarter. Make collage, clay and other art materials available for children to design their own symbolic representations of George Washington.

References:

*George Washington Word Scramble.* A to Z Teacher Stuff. Retrieved April 26, 2005, at 4:22 PM from http://www.atozteacherstuff.com/pdf. htm?scramble_washington.pdf.

While this example shows the topics for eight social studies examples with two in-depth examples, the unit incorporates activities for all areas of the curriculum—reading, writing, mathematics, science, and the arts. For in the process of "doing" social studies young children inquiring about the "big ideas" utilize the tools and concepts of other subject areas.

Another example of a thematic investigation is the often state-required exploration of community. Contrast this third-grade plan with the earlier investigation of community with four- and five-year-olds. See how the level of sophistication for the starting points has evolved. That is, third-grade teachers can count on the knowledge acquired in the years before and facilitate a deeper understanding of the underlying concepts of community.

### Chicago—How did significant events, landmarks, and individuals contribute to the history of Chicago?[4]

### Context of the Unit
This unit on Chicago will be taught after the Native American unit, which is typically taught in November.
Grade Level: 3rd

### NCSS Curriculum Strands Addressed:
1, 2, 3, 4, 5, 6, 7, 8, 9, 10

### IL Learning Strands Addressed:
Social Studies: 16, 17, and 18
Literacy: 1, 2, 3, 4, and 5
Mathematics: 6, 7, 8, 9, and 10
Other:
Science: 11, 12

Physical Education: 19, 21
F.A.: 25, 26, 27

**Core Thematic Questions:**
How did Chicago start?
How did Chicago grow?
Who were the important people in Chicago?
What were the important events in Chicago?
How did people live in Chicago long ago compared to today?
Where in Chicago did people live?
How did the Chicago fire affect life in Chicago?
What changes did the Chicago fire bring to life in Chicago?

## Key Vocabulary Taught, Applied and Assessed

Glacier, moraines, climate, swamp, Ice Age, Northwest Territory, canal, era, wetland, plain, industry, trade, homestead, manufacturing, textile, exposition, invention, immigrant, ethnic, assembly line, suffrage, union, strike, metropolis, metropolitan, sewage, typhus, cholera, reform (health reform, social reform), migration, integrated, native, segregation, violence, prohibition, "political machine," candidate, representative, architecture, symmetrical, landscape, development, racism, elevated, interstate, boomtown.

## Summary of Adaptations and Modifications for Students with Special Needs

For handouts, enlarge text on copier for students who are visually impaired.

Make a wheelchair-bound student the coach or manager of the baseball team.

Assessment practices will be read aloud.

Students will be given extra time if they need it.

Students will be allowed to pair up for written assignments.

For students who need it, questions and answers can be read aloud and written out for them. Answers can also be tape-recorded if needed.

The classroom environment will always be one of accountability with accommodations.

## Summary of Resources

Instruction books:

*Chicago* (1988) by C. Pfeiffer. Minneapolis: Dillon Press.
*Children of the Fire—Read Aloud* (1991) by R. Harriette. New York: Maxwell Macmillan.
*Journey around Chicago from A to Z* (2005) by M. D. Zschock. Beverly, MA: Commonwealth Editions.

CD-ROM: *With Open Eyes*
Musical CD-ROMs of Chicago Blues music
Frank Lloyd Wright technology CD-ROM
Videotapes on different ethnicities

## Learning Goals:

Students will understand events, trends, individuals, and movements shaping the history of Chicago, Illinois, and the United States.
Students will be able to describe and discuss the history and significant landmarks and individuals of Chicago.

## *The Chicago Unit by Week*

| | |
|---|---|
| Week 1: | General history of Chicago (introduction)—Davis book |
| Day 1: | Chapter 1: How did Chicago start? |
| Day 2: | Chapter 2: Growth of Chicago to 1893 |
| Day 4: | Chapter 3: Life in Chicago |
| Day 5: | Chapter 4: Growth of metropolis 1893–1990 |
| Week 2: | General history (continued), including chronological history of Chicago Activity: Construction of a three-dimensional skyline |
| Week 3: | General history of Chicago and biographies, with tie-ins where appropriate. Some examples of famous Chicagoans who will be studied along with their contributions are Jane Addams (community service), Percy Julian (science), Frank Lloyd Wright (architecture), Shel Silverstein (literature), and Benny Goodman (music). |
| Day 1–2: | Students will learn about biographies on Day 1. Students will choose a famous Chicagoan to write a report on. |
| Day 3–4: | Students will research and write about their famous Chicagoan. |
| Day 5: | Students will present their reports on a famous Chicagoan to their classmates. |
| Week 4: | Immigrants and present-day ethnicity |
| Day 1: | American Cultures for Children Video—Mexican American Heritage; one or two of the students volunteer to bring an authentic Mexican snack (this is a good way to get parents involved). Alternatively, invite children to bring artifacts from home that illustrate cultural heritage. |

Day 2:        American Cultures for Children Video—African American Heritage; one or two of the students volunteer to bring an authentic African American snack. Share a biography of important African American Chicagoans using http://historymakers.com (this is a project that collects oral histories and posts to the Web site).

Day 3:        American Cultures for Children Video—Chinese American Heritage; one or two of the students volunteer to bring an authentic Chinese snack. Visit the Chinese American Museum of Chicago via the Internet http://www.ccamuseum.org/. Follow up with discussion using books and borrowed artifacts.

Day 4:        American Cultures for Children Video—Irish American Heritage; one or two of the students volunteer to bring an authentic Irish snack. Invite Irish Heritage singers for presentation of traditional music. http://www.irishamhc.com/ (Irish American Heritage Center, Chicago).

Day 5:        American Cultures for Children Video—Arab American Heritage; one or two of the students volunteer to bring an authentic Arab snack. Read excerpts of *Arabs of Chicagoland* (Hanania, R. 2005, Mount Pleasant, SC: Acardia). See http://www.arcadiapublishing.com/ (Arcadia Publishing for picture/text histories of other cities and towns).

Week 5:        Migration (tie-in the pioneers)

Week 6:        Suburbs—growth from Chicago and culture in Chicago.

## Weekly Unit Statements

### Weeks 1–3

How did Chicago start? What events and conditions brought about industry, trade, and transportation? Incorporate the use of a timeline to illustrate this progression. Give a chronological history of events and individuals, specifically including trade, industry, and transportation in the shaping of Chicago.

### Weeks 4–5

Students will understand how pioneers and immigrants shaped the cultural landscape of Chicago and its effects on current ethnicities.

### Week 6

Students will be aware of how the expansion from Chicago to the suburbs took place through increased transportation and the need for more space. Focus will be placed on economic opportunities, businesses, and on small towns and farming communities and their transformation into suburbs because of growth. Using a map of metro Chicago, mark the small towns of Gurnee, Mundelein, Warrenville, Aurora, Morris, and Manteno; identify the Interstate routes near these towns, showing the links to Chicago. Then, using the yellow pages or other references, mark the shopping centers that are near these communities. Discuss the shopping center as evidence of shrinking farmland. Assign small groups of children to visit the Web sites for these communities and collect the histories. Suggest that children use census data, http://www.census.gov/, to plot on a graph the growth of each community. Each group can then prepare a community report through the decades.

## Formative Assessments

### Timeline

Each student will draw a picture of an event or person from Chicago history. The pictures will be hung around the room to construct a timeline.

### Three-Dimensional Chicago Skyline

Students will construct a model of the Chicago downtown area featuring significant landmarks and the Chicago grid.

### Math and PE Activities

Students will demonstrate cooperative learning when they perform a statistical study of Chicago baseball teams (Cubs/White Sox). They will also play a baseball game and keep track of their own player statistics as well as assess their ability to cooperate.

## Summative Assessments

### Vocabulary and Spelling Tests

Weekly vocabulary and spelling tests on words associated with the unit and specific lessons will be conducted.

### Children of the Fire

This book will be read aloud and students will be asked to write sequel chapters.

### Art Project (Can Be Both Formative and Summative)

Students will construct stained-glass windows in the style of Frank Lloyd Wright and show their understanding of symmetry, geometric shapes, and color choices.

### Ethnicity/History of Chicago

Students will construct a family timeline showing the history of their family in Chicago. This will show their understanding of chronology.

## Persuasive Writing Assessment

This will be done during the last week of the unit. Students will select a Chicago landmark that they would like to visit during their spring or summer break and write a persuasive letter to their parents to convince them to take the student to see this landmark.

## Possible Guest Speaker

Have Harriette Gillem Robinet (2001), author of *Children of the Fire* (Riverside, NJ: Aladdin) read the last two chapters aloud in person to the class. (She lives in Oak Park.)

## Possible Excursions

Chicago Historical Society—see their calendar for possible indoor excursions. (It will be too cold for outdoor activities in January–February, which is when this unit will be presented.)

## Bridges to the Rest of the Curriculum

At the beginning of the investigation of a social studies question, frequently children and teacher will use a *graphic organizer* to represent their present knowledge. In this way, both text and symbol serve to arrange concepts and thus outline what is known and what might be learned. For example, answer the question, "How do people in our city travel?" (See Graphic Organizer, Figure 10.1.)

In further investigating this topic, children graph information about the ways that their parents, and teachers, commute to work. They graph the ways that they go to buy groceries, take vacations, etc. Some additional

**Figure 8.1**
**Ways People Travel**

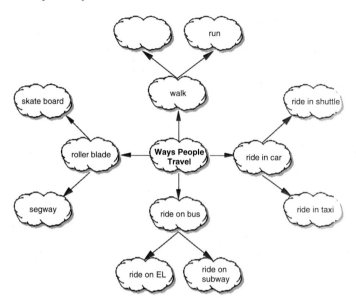

relevant mathematics standards used to investigate this and other questions follow:

In prekindergarten through Grade 2, all students should—

Formulate questions that can be addressed with data and collect, organize, and display relevant data to answer them

- pose questions and gather data about themselves and their surroundings;
- sort and classify objects according to their attributes and organize data about the objects;
- represent data using concrete objects, pictures, and graphs.

Select and use appropriate statistical methods to analyze data

- describe parts of the data and the set of data as a whole to determine what the data show.

Develop and evaluate inferences and predictions that are based on data

- discuss events related to students' experiences as likely or unlikely.

Understand and apply basic concepts of probability

(*Source*: National Council for Teachers of Mathematics, *Principles and Standards for School Mathematics*, http://standards.nctm.org)

As they investigate the topic, the children and teachers might look at the ways that grandparents traveled and think about the ways that people might travel in the future. These investigations might bridge to a question of how societies use energy (IL 11.A 1.b shown later)? The social studies aspect of the question links to the "common good" and the needs of the society through the investigation of this topic. To begin the investigation, ask children to interview grandparents or other older adults with questions such as the following:

- When you were little where did you live?
- How did you get to school?
- Where did your friends live? How did you visit them?
- How did you go to see relatives for holidays?
- Did you always live in the same place?
- How old were you when you learned to drive? Where did you go?
- Did you ever ride a bus? School bus? Subway? EL? Boat?
- Did you ever travel on a train? Fly on a plane? When?

Then, collect the interview data and make a class summary, using graphs and charts. Follow up with discussions of the history of the development of interstates. Then, collect news stories about oil production, trends in car manufacturing, availability of public transportation. Link this conversation to the "common good." Following are suggested sources for these investigations.

## Current Events

CNN: http://www.cnn.com/EDUCATION/.
MSN: http://kids.msn.com/.
Newsweek Education Program: http://www.newsweekeducation.com/index.php.
Scholastic News: http:www/scholastic.com.
Time for Kids: http://www.timeforkids.coem/TFK/.

US News Education Program: http://www.usnews.com/usnews/edu/
   k12/k12home.htm.

Weekly Reader: http://www.weeklyreader.com/.

## Books

Baylor, B. (1983). *The best town in the world*. New York: Simon & Schuster.

Castor, H. (1993). *Trucks*. Tulsa, OK: Usborne.

Crews, D. (1989). *Flying*. New York: Mulberry-Greenwillow.

Crews, D. (1993). *Freight train*. New York: Mulberry.

Crews, D. (1980). *Truck*. New York: Greenwillow Books.

Egan, T. (1995). *Chestnut cove*. Boston: Houghton Mifflin.

Heap, C. (1998). *The DK book of trains*. Pasedena, CA: DK Publishing.

Hoban, T. (1971). *I Can Read Signs*. New York: Greenwillow.

Jacobson, K. (1995). *My New York*. New York: Little Brown.

Johnstone, M. (1994). *Cars*. New York: Dorling Kindersley.

Siebert, D. (1986). *Truck song*. New York: Harper & Row.

Williams, M. (2003). *Don't let the pigeon drive the bus*. Boston: Hyperion
   Books for Children.

Zelinsky, P. O. (1990). *The wheels on the bus*. New York: Putnam.

Early grade science standards for Illinois are based on those of the National Science Teacher Association; these are stated as follows:

## Early Elementary

11.A.1a Describe an observed event.

11.A.1b Develop questions on scientific topics.

11.A.1c Collect data for investigations using measuring instruments
   and technologies.

11.A.1d Record and store data using available technologies.

11.A.1e Arrange data into logical patterns and describe the patterns.

11.A.1f Compare observations of individual and group results.

(*Source*: Illinois Learning Standards, Illinois State Board of Education.
   http://www.isbe.net)

In all of these investigations, children are reading, interpreting pictures and charts as well as summarizing data and writing or illustrating findings. These actions intersect with the requirements for teaching reading and writing as displayed in the following.

The standards for teaching the English language arts follow:

## The Standards

1. Students read a wide range of print and non-print texts to build an understanding of texts, of themselves, and of the cultures of the United States and the world; to acquire new information; to respond to the needs and demands of society and the workplace; and for personal fulfillment. Among these texts are fiction and nonfiction, classic and contemporary works.

2. Students read a wide range of literature from many periods in many genres to build an understanding of the many dimensions (e.g., philosophical, ethical, aesthetic) of human experience.

3. Students apply a wide range of strategies to comprehend, interpret, evaluate, and appreciate texts. They draw on their prior experience, their interactions with other readers and writers, their knowledge of word meaning and of other texts, their word identification strategies, and their understanding of textual features (e.g., sound–letter correspondence, sentence structure, context, graphics).

4. Students adjust their use of spoken, written, and visual language (e.g., conventions, style, vocabulary) to communicate effectively with a variety of audiences and for different purposes.

5. Students employ a wide range of strategies as they write and use different writing process elements appropriately to communicate with different audiences for a variety of purposes.

6. Students apply knowledge of language structure, language conventions (e.g., spelling and punctuation), media techniques, figurative language, and genre to create, critique, and discuss print and non-print texts.

7. Students conduct research on issues and interests by generating ideas and questions, and by posing problems. They gather, evaluate, and synthesize data from a variety of sources (e.g., print and nonprint texts, artifacts, people) to communicate their discoveries in ways that suit their purpose and audience.

8. Students use a variety of technological and information resources (e.g., libraries, databases, computer networks, video) to gather and synthesize information and to create and communicate knowledge.

9. Students develop an understanding of and respect for diversity in language use, patterns, and dialects across cultures, ethnic groups, geographic regions, and social roles.

10. Students whose first language is not English make use of their first language to develop competency in the English language arts and to develop understanding of content across the curriculum.

11. Students participate as knowledgeable, reflective, creative, and critical members of a variety of literacy communities.

12. Students use spoken, written, and visual language to accomplish their own purposes (e.g., for learning, enjoyment, persuasion, and the exchange of information).

(*Source: Standards for teaching the English language arts* (1996), International Reading Association. http://www.reading.org)

Besides using the standards from the professional associations to guide the integration of social studies subjects, check the cooperative Web site: http://www.marcopolo-education. On a fine summer June day, there were examples of integrated units for primary grades on animal habitats, looking at landmarks, quilts, "Where did the pencil come from?" In addition, the Web site contains a section on integrated teaching as well as material on standards alignment.

## Summary

In this chapter, the discussion began with highlights of the purposes of social studies in the early childhood curriculum with a focus on using the content and processes as an anchor for planning the thematic studies of instruction. Using the techniques of project-based instruction or integrated learning, teachers can accomplish the goals of social studies as well as accomplish the requirements for the development of literacy, mathematic skills and concepts, and scientific problem solving. Examples of work that teacher candidates explored for use with young children are included. Note that these examples were developed using state standards, NCSS themes, and knowledge of child interests at diverse ages. These planning efforts are a pragmatic attempt to employ a constructivist perspective while utilizing child care agency and school district mandates.

## Implications and Conclusions

Social studies as a discipline brings important content—development of self in the social world, appreciation for civic responsibility—and processes that foster lifelong learning. Planning for the inclusion of social studies contents and processes creates an opportunity for teachers and young children to appreciate the rich diverse social context in family, school, community settings. The processes of teaching and learning in social studies include all of the various data-gathering, information-processing, and data-presentation skills, knowledge, and dispositions that shape "school success" and develop citizenship.

## Activities in the Field

1. Visit a preschool classroom and a primary classroom. Look at the schedules for the days. Notice whether social studies appears in the list of planned activities. If so, ask the teacher how the planning happens for social studies. If not, using your observations, sketch some ideas for incorporating the social studies on that day.

2. In situations where you have access to young children, choose some "big ideas" to ask the children about. Include concepts like democracy, justice, discrimination, civic engagement. Notice how you explain the concepts and what the children have to say in the dialog. Develop an outline of a plan to engage children in further dialog and investigation of the big ideas.

## Activities in the Library

1. Read several issues of *Social Studies and the Young Learner.* Collect ideas for thematic unit development as well as suggested ways to incorporate the processes of social studies.

2. Read several issues of *The Horn Book.* Collect an annotated bibliography of possible children's books to use in thematic units that you might develop for a particular or broad range of ages.

## Study Questions

1. What is the history of the best way to teach social studies?

2. How do the NCSS ten themes, and the scope and sequence of NCSS, give support to developmentally appropriate practice?

3. How are the processes of social studies similar to the objectives for other content areas, for example, literacy, math, science?

4. What are some ways to begin to think about teaching social studies?

5. Why are the social studies an important content area for young children?

## Reflect and Re-read

1. How does the NCSS approach to social studies development and understanding compare to the goals and best-practice statements of NAEYC?

2. Examine the sample thematic investigations. Why and how will you use or change these in your classrooms? What improvements might you make?

3. After reading this book, what will you tell parents and administrators about the content and processes of social studies?

## Notes

1. Allison Dritz, DePaul University Early Childhood Education Teacher Candidate.

2. Marjorie B. G. Hudzik, DePaul University Teacher Candidate.

3. Mollie Sutfin & Elizabeth Borg De Paul University Teacher Candidates.

4. Sharman Galezewski and Holly Monahan, DePaul University Teacher Candidates.

## Suggested Readings

Alleman, J., & Brophy, J. (2003). *Social studies excursions K-3, Book three: Powerful units on childhood, money, and government*. Portsmouth, NH: Heinemann.

Alleman, J., & Brophy, J. (2002). *Social studies excursions K-3, Book two: Powerful units on communication, transportation and family living*. Portsmouth, NH: Heinemann.

Alleman, J., & Brophy, J. (2001). *Social studies excursions K-3, Book one: Powerful units on food, clothing, and shelter*. Portsmouth, NH: Heinemann. This series of three books shows how to develop child friendly topics in a holistic and engaging way.

Bickart, T. S., Jablon, J. R. & Dodge, D. T. (1999). *Building the primary classroom: A comprehensive guide to teaching and learning*. Washington, DC: Teaching Strategies. Find examples of ways to develop social studies in context.

Bredekamp, S., and Copple, C. (Eds.). (1997). *Developmentally appropriate practice in early childhood programs (rev. ed.)*. Washington, DC: National Association for the Education of Young Children. This is the position statement on best teaching practices and principles in early childhood.

Dodge, D. T., Colker, L., & Heroman, C. (2002). *The Creative Curriculum for Preschool* (4th ed.). Washington, DC: Teaching Strategies, Inc. Find examples of ways to develop social studies in context.

Oakes, J., & Lipton, M. (2003). *Teaching to change the world* (2nd ed.). Boston: McGraw-Hill. This book explores theoretical issues in a provocative discussion of diverse views.

Rogovin, P. (1998). *Classroom interviews: A world of learning*. Portsmouth, NH: Heinemann.

Rogovin, P. (2001). *The research workshop: Bringing the world into your classroom.* Portsmouth, NH: Heinemann. These two books by Rogovin are examples of ways to engage children in the processes of social studies to further development.

Seefeldt, C. (2005). *How to work with standards in the early childhood classroom.* New York: Teachers College. This book takes teachers from theory to practice in the use of standards.

Seefeldt, C., & Galper, A. (2006). *Active experiences for active children: Social studies* (2nd ed.). Upper Saddle River, NJ: Prentice-Hall/Merrill. Find examples of activities and suggestions for planning in this book.

Sobel, D. (1998). *Mapmaking with children: Sense of place education for the elementary years.* Portsmouth, NH: Heinemann. This book shows how to use mapmaking across the curriculum.

Winston, L. (1997). *Keepsakes: Using family stories in elementary classrooms.* Portsmouth, NH: Heinemann. Learn how to use family stories to develop historical skills and understandings.

## References

Hanania, A. (2005). *Arabs of Chicagoland.* Chicago: Arcadia Publishing.

Katz, L. G., & Chard, S. C. (2000). *Engaging children's minds: The project approach in education* (2nd ed). Stamford, CT: Ablex.

Maxim, G. W. (2006). *Dynamic social studies for constructivist classrooms: Inspiring tomorrow's social scientists.* Upper Saddle River, NJ: Merrill.

Mindes, G., & Donovan, M. (2001). *Building character: Five enduring themes for a stronger early childhood curriculum.* Needham Heights, MA: Allyn & Bacon.

National Council for Social Studies. (1984). In search for a scope and sequence for social studies. *Social Education, 48*(4), 376–385.

National Council for Social Studies. (1994). *Curriculum standards for social studies: Expectations for excellence.* Washington, DC: National Council for Social Studies.

Washington, G. (1789). *Message to Catholics.* Referenced in Seldes, G. (1960). *The great quotations.* A Caesar-Stuart book. New York: Stuart.

### Children's Literature

Bartoletti, S. C., & Nivola, C. A. (2004) *The flag maker.* Wilmington, MA: Houghton Mifflin.

Braver, V. (2004) *Pinky promise: A book about telling the truth.* Washinton, DC: Child & Family Press.

Brimer, L. D., & Trip, C. T. (2003) *A flag for all.* Danbury, CT: Children's Press.

Brown, M. W. (1993) *Little fireman.* New York: HarperCollins.

Chandra, D., & Comora, M. (2003) *George Washington's teeth.* Gordonsville, VA: Farrar, Strauss, & Giroux.

Crampton, W. D., & Crampton, W. (2003) *Flags of the world.* Tulsa, OK: Usborne Books.

Crews, D. (1984). *School bus.* New York: Green Willow.

Douglas, L. G. (2003) *The Statue of Liberty.* Danbury, CT: Children's Press.

Fanelli, S. (1995). *My map book.* New York: HarperCollins.

Fritz, J. (1998) *George Washington's breakfast.* New York: Putnam.

Gross, R. B. (1993) . . .*If you grew up with George Washington.* New York: Scholastic.

Heilbroner, J. (2001) *Meet George Washington.* New York: Random House.

Henry, H. F. (2004) *What freedom means to me.* Woodland Hills, CA: Cubbie Blues.

Herman, J. (1998) *Red, white and blue: The story of the American flag.* New York: Penquin.

Jaeggi, C., & Seltzer, M. (1995) *I know about flags.* Chicago: Rand McNally.

Kalman, B. (1998). *Community helpers from A to Z.* New York: Crabtree Publishing.

Knowlton, L. (2002) *Red, white, and blue.* Dallas: Pelican.

Krasilovsky, P. (2003) *Benny's flag.* Lanham, MD: Roberts Rinehart Publishers.

Liebman, D. (2002). *I want to be a doctor.* Toronto: Firefly.

Osbourne, M. P. (2000) *Magic treehouse #22: Revolutionary War on Wednesday.* New York: Random House.

*The pledge of allegiance.* (2000). New York: Scholastic.

Prince, A. J., & Paley, J. (2004) *Meet our flag, old glory.* Collingdale, PA: DIANE.

Rosen, M. (1989). *We're going on a bear hunt.* New York: Margaret K. McElderry Books.

St. George, J. (2005) *Take the lead, George Washington.* East Rutherford, NJ: Philomel.

St. George, J. (2000) *You want to be president.* New York: Putnam.

Steele, C. (1995) *I wonder why countries fly flags and other questions about people and places.* Helena, MT: Kingfisher.

Wallner, A. (1998) *Betsy Ross.* New York: Holiday House.

Waters, K. (1992) *The story of the White House.* New York: Scholastic.

Woods, A. (1997) *Young George Washington: America's first president.* Mahwah, NJ: Troll.

Woodruff, E. (1993) *George Washington's socks.* New York: Scholastic.

## Web Sites

International Reading Association: http://www.reading.org. Many articles on teaching reading and the language arts are available on this site as well as links to additional resources.

MarcoPolo Education: http://www.marcopolo-education.org. This Web site is a consortium of national and international organizations that provides many examples of integrated teaching lessons and units. Standards are an integral part of the lesson samples.

National Council for Social Studies: http://www.ncss.org. Check this site for position statements on social studies teaching as well as practical resources for planning.

National Council for Teachers of Mathematics: http://www.nctm.org. The Web site shows resources for teaching problem solving, geometry, linking math to literacy, among other current issues.

National Science Teacher Association: http://www.nsta.org. The Web site illustrates ways to teach science topics and links to science teaching resources.

# Children's Literature Organized by National Council of Social Studies Themes

Prepared by Nichole Meier, School of Education Graduate Assistant, DePaul University, Chicago

## Culture

*Coming to America: A Muslim Family's Story* by Bernard Wolf. Lee & Low Books. 2003. 44 pp. The story of an immigrant Muslim family's experience living in New York City. Illustrated through photos. Grades 2–5.

*Hachiko: The True Story of a Loyal Dog* by Pamela S Turner, illustrated by Yan Nascimbene. Houghton Mifflin. 2004. 32 pp The story of an animal hero, Hachiko, and the dedicated monument. Illustrates Japanese culture and ideas of local and national heroes. Grades: Pre-K–3.

*The Hatseller and the Monkeys* by Baba Wague Diakite. Scholastic Press. 1999. 32 pp. A West African version of *Caps for Sale*. The folktale is transformed using an African setting and words. Grades K–3.

*Hannah Is My Name* written and illustrated by Belle Yang. Candlewick Press. 2004. 32 pp. Set in the late 1960s, Hannah, a young Taiwanese girl, immigrates to San Francisco's Chinatown. A child's point of view on both the joy and trials of immigration. Grades K–3.

*Home at Last* by Susan Middleton Elya, illustrated By Felipe Davalos. Lee & Low Books. 2002. 32 pp. The story of an immigrant family from Mexico living in the United States. A young girl adjusts to school as her parents learn to navigate life in the United States. Includes Spanish text. Grades K–3.

*Mei Mei Loves the Morning* by Margaret Holloway Tsubakiyama, illustrated by Cornelius Van Wright and Ying-Hwa Hu. Albert Whitman. 1999. 32 pp. A young girl and her grandfather's morning routine in urban China. Grades Pre K–2.

## Time, Continuity, and Change

*Century Farm: One Hundred Years on a Family Farm* by Cris Peterson, illustrated with photos by Alvis Upitis. Boyds Mill Press. 1999. 32 pp. A photographic journey of a family dairy farm in Wisconsin. Describes the day-to-day operations and the family's history. Grades K–3.

*Circle Unbroken* by Margot Thesis Raven, illustrated by E. B. Lewis. Melanie Kroupa Books/Farrar, Straus, and Giroux Books for Young Readers. 2004. 48 pp. An African American girl in South Carolina learns the history of her grandmother's sweet grass basket weaving and its roots in slavery. Historical note and bibliography appended. Grades K–5.

*George Washington's Teeth* by Deborah Chandra and Madeleine Comora, illustrated by Brock Cole. Farrar, Straus and Giroux. 2003. 40 pp. An examination of early American history through a focus on George Washington's teeth. Written in rhyming verse. Grades K–3.

*Grandma Moses,* written and illustrated by Alexandra Wallner. 2004. Holiday House. 32 pp. Biographical introduction to the life of Anna Mary Robertson, better known as Grandma Moses. Illustrations are in the Grandma Moses/early American style. Grades K–3.

*The Great Expedition of Lewis and Clark: By Private Reubin Field, Member of the Corps of Discovery* by Judith Edwards, illustrated by Sally Wern Comport. Farrar, Straus and Giroux. 2003. 40 pp. A narrative account of the Lewis and Clark expedition written in journal form by Private Reubin Field. Book contains actual quotes from Lewis and Clark's journals and letters. Grades 2–5.

*Home,* written and illustrated by Jeannie Baker. Greenwillow Books. 2004. 32 pp. A wordless book that follows the change of an urban neighborhood during one girl's life from birth to motherhood. Highlights the role a community plays in revitalizing a neighborhood. Grades K–3.

*The Little House* by Virginia Lee Burton. Houghton Mifflin. 1978. 44 pp. The story of a rural house that becomes engulfed by urban sprawl over the years. Grades Pre-K–2.

## People, Places, and Environments

*A Cool Drink of Water* by Barbara Kerely. National Geographic Children's Books. 2002. 32 pp. Full-page photos with minimal text about water gathering around the world and the importance of water to human life. Grades Pre-K–2.

*Candy Shop* by John Wahl, illustrated by Nicole Wong. Charlesbridge. 2004. 32 pp. An ethnically diverse urban neighborhood deals with intolerance when someone scrawls hurtful words (not shown) on the sidewalk of Miz Chu's candy shop. Daniel, an African American boy, and his community triumph over hate. Grades 1–3.

*Going North* by Janice Harrington, illustrated by Jerome Lagarrigue. Melanie Kroupa Books/Farrar, Straus, and Giroux Books for Young Readers. 2004. 40 pp. The story of an African American family's migration north in the 1960s. The family stops at "Negro Only" gas stations and stores on their way north seeking better jobs and schools. Grades 3–5.

*Henry Works*, written and illustrated by D. B Johnson. Houghton Mifflin. 2004. 32 pp. Henry (Henry David Thoreau) goes to "work"; a walk in the woods where he observes nature's details and helps neighbors and the environment. Includes biographical information on Henry David Thoreau. Grades Pre-K–K.

*Hide and Sneak* by Michael Kusugak, illustrated by Vladyana Krykorka. Annick Press. 1992. 32 pp. In this tale, a young girl plays hide and seek in the artic tundra. An introduction to Artic landscape, cultures, and folktales. Grades K–3.

*High as a Hawk: A Brave Girl's Historic Climb* by T. A. Barron, illustrated by Ted Lewin. Philomel Books. 2004. 32 pp. Based on the historic story of 8-year-old Harriet Logan who in 1905 was the youngest person ever to climb Longs Peak in Colorado. Includes author's note. Grades 1–3.

*I Read Signs* by Tanya Hoban. HarperTrophy. 1987. 32 pp. Photographs of thirty familiar signs found in a children's community. Grades Pre-K–K.

*Our World: A Child's First Picture Atlas* by the National Geographic Society. National Geographic Children's Books. 2000. 32 pp. A first atlas for children. Introduction to geography and map concepts. Grades Pre-K–1.

*Squirrel and John Muir*, written and illustrated by Emily Arnold McCully. Farrar, Straus, and Giroux Books for Young Readers. 2004. 40 pp. The story of the naturalist John Muir and his pupil relationship with his employer's young daughter, Floy Hutchings. The setting is Yosemite Valley in the late 19th century. The author explains more about Muir's later work, such as helping to establish Yosemite national Park and founding the Sierra Club. Grades K–3.

## Individual Development and Identity

*Beautiful Blackbird* by Ashley Bryan. Athenaeum. 2003. 40 pp. A rhythmic adaptation of a Zambian tale that introduces ideas of identity, differences, and community. Grades Pre-K–2.

*The Boy on Fairfield Street: How Ted Geisel Grew Up to Become Dr. Seuss* by Kathleen Krull, illustrated by Steve Johnson and Lou Fancher. Random House Children's Books. 2004. 48 pp. A biographical look at Dr. Seuss's life from early childhood to young adulthood. How Seuss became Seuss. Grades 3 and up.

*Brave Harriet: The First Woman to Fly the English Channel* by Marissa Moss, illustrated by C. F. Payne. Silver Whistle. 2001. 32 pp. The story of Harriet Quimby, the first woman to fly solo across the English Channel in 1912. However, her accomplishment was overshadowed by the sinking of the Titanic. Grades K–3.

*Hope* by Isabell Monk and illustrated by Janice Lee Porter. Carolhoda Books. 1998. 32 pp. A young girl learns her about her namesake and biracial heritage. The story reflects on the histories of her immigrant and slave ancestors. Grades K–3.

*Knockin' on Wood: Starring Peg Leg Bates*, written and illustrated by Lynne Barasch. Lee & Low Books. 2004. 32 pp. The story of Clayton "Peg Leg" Bates, who, despite his leg amputation at age 12, pursued a successful career in vaudeville as a tap dancer. Story deals with ideas of racism in America during the early twentieth century. Grades 2–3.

*Love to Mama: A Tribute to Mothers* by Pat Mora (Ed.), illustrated by Paula S. Barragan. Lee & Low Books; Bilingual edition. 2004. 32 pp. Collection of poems written by thirteen Latino poets that pays tribute to mothers and grandmothers. Grades 3 and up.

*Rainy Day* by Emma Haughton, illustrated by Angelo Rinaldi. Lerner Publications. 2004. 32 pp. The story of a relationship between a boy and his father after a divorce. The boy is visiting his father at his father's new apartment and the weather has spoiled their plans. Grades K–2.

## Individuals, Groups, and Institutions

*Amish Horses*, by Richard Ammon, illustrated by Pamela Patrick. Athenaeum. 2001. 40 pp. A story of horses and people and their life on an Amish farm in Pennsylvania. Introduction to Amish life. Grades 1–3.

*The Bully Blockers Club* by Teresa Bateman, illustrated by Jackie Urbanovic. Albert Whitman. 2004. 32 pp. Lotty Raccoon devises a plan to stop the class bully: the Bully Blockers Club. A great springboard for discussions on bullying in the classroom. Teacher's Notes. Grades Pre-K–3.

*The Color of Us* by Karen Katz. Owlet Paperbacks. 2002. 32 pp. Lena and her mother walk through the neighborhood and reflect on all the shades of skin color in their neighborhood. Grades Pre-K–2.

*The Eagle and the Wren* by Jane Goodall, illustrated by Alexander Reichstein. Michael Neugebauer Book. 2002. 40 pp. Conservationist Jane Goodall tells the story of a contest to see who can fly the highest. The overall message highlights the idea of teamwork. Grades Pre-K–3.

*Lots of Grandparents* by Shelley Rotner and Shelia M. Kelly (Ed.D), illustrated with photographs by Shelly Rotner. Millbrook Press. 32 pp. A pictorial look at culturally diverse groups of grandparents in many settings doing different activities. The word for grandparents is introduced in seven different languages. Grades Pre-K–1.

*Mommy Far, Mommy Near: An Adoption Story* by Carol Antoinette Peacock, illustrated by Shawn Costello Brownell. Albert Whitman. 2000. 32 pp. The story of Elizabeth, a young Chinese girl who was adopted by a Caucasian North American family. Elizabeth comes to terms with adoption and having two mothers; one near and one far. Grades Pre-K–3.

## Power, Authority, and Governance

*One of the Problems of Everett Anderson* by Lucille Clifton, illustrated by Ann Grifalconi. Henry Holt. 2001. 32 pp. Everett's new friend Greg comes to school with bruises and scars. Addresses the issue of child abuse. Grades K–3.

*Red, White, Blue, and Uncle Who?: The Story Behind Some of America's Patriotic Symbols* by Teresa Bateman, illustrated by John O'Brien. Holiday House. 2001. 64 pp. Seventeen different patriot symbols and sites are presented, with relevant facts and information. "Symbols" include the flag, Uncle Sam, Mount Rushmore, and the Pledge of Allegiance. Grades 3–6.

*Sequoyah: The Cherokee Man Who Gave His People Writing,* written and illustrated by James Rumford. Translated by Anna Sixkiller Huckaby. Houghton Mifflin. 2004. 32 pp. The story of Sequoyah, the Cherokee man that invented the written form of the language in early 1800s. Translated into Cherokee. Grades 1–3.

*Stars and Stripes: The Story of the American Flag* by Sarah L. Thompson, illustrated by Bob Dacey and Debra Bandelin. HarperCollins. 2003. 32 pp. Reviews the history of the American flag and how it has changed during different political events. Introduces the flag and U.S. history. Grades 1–3.

## Production, Distribution, and Consumption

*Everybody Works* by Shelly Rotner and Ken Keisler, photos by Shelly Rotner. Millbrook Press. 2003. 32 pp. Large colorful photos depict men and women in conventional and unconventional jobs. Author acknowledges different kinds of work: earning money, volunteering, and hobbies as work. Grades Pre-K–K.

*Harvest* by George Ancona. Illustrated with photos. Marshall Cavendish. 2001. 48 pp. Photo-documentary of Mexican migrant farm workers on the west coast. Includes personal narratives of the workers and information on harvesting. Information on Cesar Chavez included. Grades 3 and up.

*Margaret Knight, Girl Inventor* by Marlene Targ Brill, illustrated by Joanne Friar. Millbrook Press. 2001. 32 pp. The story of Margaret Knight, a young girl who worked in a textile mill and at the age of 12 invented a safety device on weaving looms that saved lives. Grades 2–5.

*Recycle! A Handbook for Kids* by Gail Gibbons. Little, Brown. 1992. 32 pp. Discusses the recycling process starting with the landfill and inspires kids to recycle. Gives facts/statistics on consumption and waste. A concluding page gives suggestions on how kids can make a difference. Grades 2–4.

*Supermarket* by Kathleen Krull, illustrated by Melanie Hope Greenberg. Holiday House. 2001. 32 pp. A behind-the-scenes look at the neighborhood grocery store. Filled with facts about food consumption and productions. Grades Pre-K–3.

## Science, Technology, and Society

*Building a House* by Byron Barton. HarperTrophy. 1990. 32 pp. The story of how a house is built. Simple text follows each step of construction. Grades Pre-K–K.

*Harbor* by Doanld Crews. HarperTrophy. 1987. 32 pp. A picture book that shows a busy harbor full of different types of boats. Grades Pre-K–1.

*Hard Hat Area,* written and illustrated by Susan L. Roth. Bloomsbury Children's Books. 40 pp. A step-by-step look at the construction of a skyscraper in New York. The story follows Kristen, an ironwork apprentice, through her typical day. Author's note included about the real Kristen. Grades 1–3.

*On the Same Day in March: A Tour of the World's Weather* by Marilyn Singer, illustrated by Frane Lessac. HarperTrophy. 2002. 40 pp. A description of the weather in seventeen different locales around the world, ranging from urban areas to countrysides. Grades K–2.

*Sergio and the Hurricane* by Alexandra Wallner. Henry Holt and Company. 2000. 32 pp. Sergio lives in San Juan Puerto Rico and a hurricane is coming. The tale follows the hurricane and the aftermath of rebuilding. Grades Pre-K–2.

## Global Connections

*A Pride of African Tales* by Donna L. Washington, illustrated by James Ransome. HarperCollins Children's Books. 2004. 80 pp. A collection of tales from throughout Africa. Demonstrates the richness and diversity of the continent and the importance of storytelling. Grades 2–5.

*Be My Neighbor*, written and illustrations/photographs by Maya Ajmera and John D. Ivanko. Charlesbridge. 2004. 32 pp. An exploration of neighborhoods from around the world. Explores the similarities and diversity in communities. Grades Pre-K–3.

*It's Back to School We Go* by Ellen Jackson, illustrated by Jan Davey Ellis. Millbrook Press. 2003. 32 pp. Introduction to the school experiences of children from eleven different countries. Grades 1–4.

*To Be an Artist* by Maya Ajmera and John D. Ivanko. Illustrated with photographs. Charlesbridge. 2004. 32 pp. Photos depict children from around the world defining "art" through drawing singing, writing, acting, sculpting, playing instruments, making crafts, and painting. Map. Grades K–3.

## Civic Ideals and Practices

*Henry and the Kite Dragon* by Bruce Edward Hall, illustrated by William Low. Philomel Books. 2004. 40 pp. Two groups of children, one from Chinatown and the other from Little Italy, clash in this story set in 1920s New York City. The children come to a peaceful compromise and form friendships despite their differences. Grades Pre-K–4.

*Martin's Big Words: The Life of Dr. Martin Luther King, Jr.* by Doreen Rappaport, illustrated by Brian Collier. Jump at the Sun. 2001. 40 pp. A pictorial biography of the leader and his work. Includes text and quotes from King's speeches and writings. Grades K–3.

*Pete for President* by Daisy Alberto, illustrated by Blanche Sims. Kane Press. 2004. 32 pp. A look at the electoral process when two third-grade classmates run for class president. Introduces key vocabulary in the election process. Grades 2–3.

*Rivka's First Thanksgiving* by Elsa Okon Rael, illustrated by Maryann Kovalski. Aladdin. 2004. 32 pp. Riva learns about Thanksgiving at school and convinces her Jewish immigrant family and Rabbi to celebrate the holiday. Set in New York's Lower East Side in 1910. Grades 1–3.

*When Esther Morris Headed West: Women, Wyoming, and the Right to Vote* by Connie Nordhielm Wooldridge, illustrated by Jacqueline Rogers. Holiday House. 2001. 32 pp. The story of Esther Morris, suffragist, who pushed for gender equality in Wyoming. She was an experienced voter and Justice of the Peace by 1870. Grades 2–5.

# Index

activities to facilitate children's understanding of the world and its structure, 42
Alleman & Brophy, 46, 85, 95
additive approach, 71
anecdotal records, 139
antibias curriculum, 72–73
assessing achievement in social studies: issue of the pervasive influence of culture, 74
assessment, 13; authentic, 136; choosing method to fit the purpose of learning, 139

backward design, 131
Banks, 29, 71
baseline, 22, 104
benchmarks, 131
Berry & Mindes, 22, 26, 105
best practice as described by National Learned Societies, 42
beyond tolerance to awareness of the wider world, 72
Bickart, Jablon, & Dodge, 48
big events, 50
big ideas, 40–41, 52, 102, 145
big picture, 86, 131, 140
Bredekamp & Copple, 6, 42, 46, 159

Bredekamp & Rosengrant, 12
broader arena of teaching social studies: beyond tolerance to awareness of the wider world, 72
Bruner, 68

character education, 30–33
checklists, 140
Center for Media Literacy, 114
children's literature, 21, 33, 52, 109
Chicago, 108
civic ideals and practices, 44, 103
classroom community building, 22
classroom culturally responsive content, 67
classroom provisions that model respect and build a sense of community, 26
cognitive reciprocity, 32
cognitive self-concept, 21
"common good," the, 29–30
community building, 22
concentric circles approach, 81
concept loading, 120
conflict resolution, 27, 42
constructivist, 14
content integration, 72
contributions approach, 71

context, 7, 10, 11, 67
criterion-referenced assessment, 140
cultural contributions in the investigation of social studies, 10
culturally relevant pedagogy and issues of "hidden curricula," 13, 27
culture, 10–13, 61
culture as theme, 102
culture, context, and meaning, 63
curricular mapping, 131
curriculum of the social studies, the, 4

Darling-Hammond, 8
Davey, 5, 8–9, 79
De Gaetano, Williams, & Volk, 11, 62
dealing with the effect of environmental stress, 92
developmentally appropriate practice, 6, 42
DeVries, Hildebrant, & Zan, 22, 25, 26, 32
Dewey, 86
digital divide, 117
disappearance of social studies content in favor of reading, the, 53
disciplines based approach, 80
divergent thought, 93
diverse perspectives on classroom practices, 80
division on early childhood, 43
dynamic-themes-based approach, 81

education for the exceptional and culturally different, 70
education is multicultural and social reconstruction's emergent literacy, 52
emergent, meaningful study of the concept of a community, 86
empathy, 21, 27, 32
empowering school culture and structure, 73
enacting standards through cultural awareness, 69
English language learners, 133

environmental stress, 92
equity pedagogy, 73
ethical implications for teachers in the press for accountability, 30
etiquette, 24–25
examination of video, computer instruction and mass media, and the changing nature of school, 112
expository text process skills, 103

field trips, 51, 105, 111–12
formative, 129, 173
Fromberg, 4, 6–7, 79, 86
functional language, 53

Gay, 66
Gestwicki, 139
global connections, 44, 103
global education, 72–73
global perspectives, 82
grades, 142
graphic organizer, 120
grounding for the theme-based/problem-based curricula, 46

headstart outcomes, 70
hidden curriculum, 31
higher-order thinking, 146
high-stakes tests, 54
historical role of social studies in early childhood education, 40
holiday-based approaches, 79
human relations, 70

Illinois learning goals, 153–154, 158, 164, 166, 171, 177
individual development and identity, 44, 103
individuals, groups, and institutions, 44, 103
informal conferences with students, 141
information access, 117
integrate the social studies into the curriculum, 102, 113

integrated curriculum, 44
International Society for Technology Education, 112
issues of equity and power related to media, 110

Katz & Chard, 86, 159
knowledge construction, 72
learning centers, 48, 104
lickona, 25, 32
looking at teacher planning for social studies, 85

managing the scarcity of time in the day/year of a child, 56
map making, 51
mastery learning, 140
maxim, 3, 146
media Literacy, 117
Mindes, 13, 40–41
Mindes & Donovan, 22, 32, 147–49
multicultural and social reconstructionist, 70
multicultural approaches, 61, 71
multicultural education, 70
multicultural perspectives, 69
multicultural perspectives and approaches to social studies: enacting standards through cultural awareness, 69
multiple data source, 129, 139

National Association for Multicultural Education, 43
National Association for the Education of Young Children, 112
National Council for the Social Studies, 3, 7, 41, 96, 103, 110, 146
New York, 108
No Child Left Behind, 141
norm-referenced, 141

observation, 139
organizing the study of social studies from themes and problems, 41

parent conferences, 141

parents as part of the assessment process, 138
people, places, and environments, 44, 102
performance assessment, 136
picture files, 83
planning for the big picture, 94
portfolios, 137
postmodern, 81
post-modern-based approach, 79
power, authority, and governance, 44, 103
power of social studies in the early childhood curriculum, the, 13
practical examples of curricular implementation at the preschool and primary levels, 159–79
preschool years, 146
prejudice reduction, 73
primary years, 21, 148
production, distribution, and consumption, 44, 103
project-based learning, 45
prop boxes, 101, 108
providing a supportive structure to develop social skills, 26

questionnaires, 140

Ramsey, 11
rating scales, 140
readability, 120
reference materials, 110
report cards, 142
reporting to stakeholders, 141
ritualized holiday-centered curriculum, 80
Rogoff, 12
rubric development, 136–38
rubrics, 136
rules and structure to support learning, 13
Ryan & Bohlin, 31–33

Scaffold, 8, 20, 30, 32, 41
science, technology and society, 44, 103
school self, 20–21

scope and sequence, 44–46, 146
screening instruments, 140
Seefeldt, 111–12
self-concept and the evolution of social studies, 20
self-efficacy, 21, 27, 30
self-esteem, 20–21, 30
setting the stage for learning: building an environment to integrate the social studies into the curriculum, 102
Shanahan, 119
single-group studies, 70
Sleeter & Grant, 71
social action approach, the, 72
social content in favor of reading, 53
social justice, 73
social knowing, 1
social studies defined, 3
social studies explored, 2
social studies themes of the NCSS, 44, 103
stakeholders, 138
standards, 43–45, 47, 96, 131, 146
standardized measures in the process, 141

study of how environmental change influences peoples' lives, 89
study of transportation, 83–84
summative, 137

teacher's commands, rule statements and time-out directives, 24
textbooks, 121–23, 146
thematic strands of social studies, 151
theme-based approach, 43, 50–51
theme-based content, 41
time, continuity, and change, 44, 102
toys, texts, literature, symbols, and classroom equipment in the lives of young children, 108
transformational approach, 71
typical preschool social studies themes, 50, 149

using assessment for goal setting, 131

ways to involve children in assessment, 133
webbing, 88
Wiggins & McTighue, 131
Williams, Leslie R., 11, 61, 63,

**About the Author**

GAYLE MINDES is Professor of Education at DePaul University in Chicago.